# of Content-Area Vocabulary

Authors

Timothy Rasinski, Ph.D.

Nancy Padak, Ed.D.

Rick M. Newton, Ph.D.

Evangeline Newton, Ph.D.

Publishing Credits

Robin Erickson, *Production Director*; Lee Aucoin, *Creative Director*; Timothy J. Bradley, *Illustration Manager*; Sara Johnson, M.S.Ed., *Editorial Director*; Jennifer Viñas, *Editor*; Grace Alba, *Designer*; Corinne Burton, M.A.Ed., *Publisher*

Image Credits

All images Shutterstock

Standards

Shell Education
5301 Oceanus Drive
Huntington Beach, CA 92649-1030
http://www.shelleducation.com

ISBN 978-1-4258-0863-1

Printed by: **51307**
Printed In: **USA**
PO#: 11060

Table of Contents

Management

Lessons

Unit I—Social Studies Roots

Table of Contents

Content-Area Vocabulary Research and Practice

Content learning is largely conceptual. Words are labels for content-area concepts. Although learning these words is critical to student success, teaching them can be challenging. Asking students to look words up in their dictionaries or glossaries and then to memorize definitions provides, at best, a short-term solution. In this book, we present a systematic and research-based alternative to vocabulary learning: a roots approach. Because most words are defined (and spelled) by what their parts mean, students can expand their vocabularies by learning how words are built from the roots up. Over 90 percent of all academic vocabulary derives from Latin or Greek roots (prefixes, suffixes, bases). Moreover, when new academic words are added to English, they too are often derived from Latin and Greek roots. The logic goes like this: learning roots helps students learn content vocabulary; one root can help students unlock the meaning of multiple words. Knowing content vocabulary helps students comprehend and learn social studies, science, and mathematics.

Over 90 percent of all academic vocabulary derives from Latin or Greek roots.

The units in this book center on common roots (prefixes and bases) in science, social studies, and mathematics. We present over 15 prefixes and bases that generate over 200 words from content-area vocabulary.

What Does Research Say About Using a Roots Approach?

The size and depth of elementary students' vocabulary is associated with proficiency in reading comprehension. Effective vocabulary instruction results in higher levels of reading comprehension (Baumann et al. 2002; Beck, Perfetti, and McKeown 1982; Kame'enui, Carnine, and Freschi 1982; Stahl and Fairbanks 1986).

Morphological analysis (e.g., via a roots approach) is important because it is generative and allows students to make connections among semantically-related words or word families (Nagy and Scott 2000). In fact, developing morphological awareness is an integral component of word learning for young children (Biemiller and Slonim 2001). In a comprehensive review of 16 studies analyzing the effect of instruction in morphological awareness on literacy achievement, Carlisle (2010) observes that "children learn morphemes as they learn language" (465).

Classroom-based studies have demonstrated the effectiveness of teaching word parts and context clues in the primary and intermediate grades (Baumann et al. 2002; Baumann et al. 2005; Biemiller 2005; Carlisle 2000; Kieffer and Lesaux 2007; Mountain 2005; Porter-Collier 2010). Research in content-area vocabulary has demonstrated the effectiveness of teaching Greek and Latin word roots, especially for struggling readers (Harmon et al. 2005).

Content-Area Vocabulary Research and Practice *(cont.)*

No single instructional method is sufficient. Teachers need a variety of methods that teach word meanings while also increasing the depth of word knowledge (Blachowicz et al. 2006; Lehr, Osborn, and Hiebert 2004). These methods should aim at fostering:

Immersion

Students need frequent opportunities to use new words in diverse oral and print contexts in order to learn them thoroughly (Blachowicz and Fisher 2006).

Metacognitive and metalinguistic awareness

Students must understand and know how to manipulate the structural features of language (Nagy and Scott 2000).

Word consciousness

Word exploration (e.g., etymology) and word play (e.g., puns, riddles, games) help students develop an awareness of and interest in words (Graves and Watts-Taffe 2002, Lehr et al. 2004).

Content-Area Vocabulary Research and Practice *(cont.)*

What Is a Root?

A *root* is a word part that contains meaning and not merely sound. Roots are vocabulary multipliers—each root taught helps students discover the meanings of multiple words. There are three categories of roots, depending on their placement within a word:

prefix

A root at the beginning of a word. For example, in the word *retraction*, the initial *re-* is a prefix, meaning "back," "again."

base

The core root, which provides a word with its basic meaning. In the word *retraction*, the base is *tract*, which means "pull," "draw," "drag."

suffix

A root that ends a word. In the word *retraction*, the final *-ion* is a suffix, meaning "act of," "state of."

Note: The term *affix*, used in the Common Core State Standards, refers to either prefixes or suffixes. *Affix* contains an assimilated form of the prefix *ad-*, which means "to," "toward," or "add to." And the Latin base *fix-* means "fasten" or "stick." So an *affix* is a part of a word "added or fixed to" a base word either in front (prefix) or at the end (suffix).

What Do Prefixes and Suffixes Do?

A prefix serves one of three functions:

- A prefix can *negate* a word by meaning "not." The most common negating prefixes are *un-* (e.g., *unhappy, unwashed*) and negative *in-, im-, il-* (e.g., *invisible, impossible, illegal*). Some directional prefixes can also be negating. For example, the prefix variations *di-, dis-, dif-*, which mean "apart," "in different directions," can also mean "not." (*dis*similar = "not similar"; a *dif*ficult task is "not" easy.)
- A prefix can be *directional*: It sends the base of a word in a specific direction. The prefix *ex-* means "out," *re-* means "back," "again," *sub-* means "under," "below," and *ad-* means "to," "toward," "add to." For example, an *ex*it sign indicates the way "out" of a building; we *de*scend a staircase when we go "down"; when class *con*venes, it comes "together"; when class is *dis*missed, students scatter "in different directions"; when they *pro*ceed to their buses, they move "forward," "ahead" to their bus stops.
- A prefix can have *intensifying force,* meaning "very," "thoroughly." A *per*fectly baked cake, for example, is "thoroughly" done. Quantitative and numerical prefixes are also intensifying.

A suffix changes the part of speech (e.g., *act, action; swift, swiftly*) or modifies the base (e.g., *fast, faster*).

Vocabulary Research and Practice *(cont.)*

What Is Assimilation?

Some prefixes have multiple forms because of an easily recognizable and predictable phenomenon called *assimilation*. Assimilation simply means that some consonants at the beginning of a word change and become like ("similar to" = assimilate) the consonants that follow them. For example, the prefix *con-* occurs in the words *convention* and *conference*. Through assimilation, it also appears in *collect*, *commotion*, and *correct*. The reason is simple: assimilation makes a word easier to pronounce (consider *conlect* vs. *collect*). Although assimilation causes spelling changes, the meaning of the prefix does not change.

While this concept does not apply directly to all of the lessons in this book, as your students become more "roots" aware, they may raise questions about why the spelling of some prefixes change. The following information will help answer these questions.

Latin Prefixes that Assimilate

Prefix	Meaning	Examples
ad-	to, toward, add to	*admit, accelerate, affect, aggravate, allusion, appendix, arrogant, assimilate, attract*
con-, co-	with, together, very	*congregate, coworker, collect, combine, commit, compose, correct*
ex-, e-, ef-	out, from, completely	*expose, edict, effect*
dis-, di-, dif-	apart, in different directions, not	*disintegrate, divert, different, difficult*
in-, im-, il- (directional)	in, on, into, against	*induct, insert, imbibe, immigrant, import, impose, illustrate*
in-, im-, il- (negative)	not	*infinite, insatiable, ignoble, illegal, illegible, impossible, irresponsible*
ob-	toward, up against	*obstruct, occurrence, offensive, oppose*
sub-	under, up from under	*submarine, succeed, suffer, support, suspend*

Vocabulary Research and Practice *(cont.)*

Types of Assimilation

Unassimilated Prefixes

We can easily pronounce the unaltered prefix with the base. Hence, there is no need to assimilate.

con + vention = convention	*ob + struction = obstruction*
in + visible = invisible	*ex + pose = expose*
sub + terranean = subterranean	*dis + tract = distract*

Partial Assimilation

We cannot easily pronounce *n* when it is followed by such consonants as *b, p,* and (occasionally) *f.* In such cases, the final *n* of the prefix partially assimilates into *m.*

in + possible = impossible	*con + bine = combine*
con + pose = compose	*con + fort = comfort*

Full Assimilation

We cannot easily pronounce these unaltered prefixes when followed by certain consonants. In such cases, the final consonant of the prefix changes into the initial consonant of the base that follows it. The result is a doubled consonant near the beginning.

con + rect = correct	*ex + fect = effect*
in + legal = illegal	*dis + fer = differ*
sub + fer = suffer	*ad + similation = assimilation*
ob + pose = oppose	

Vocabulary Research and Practice *(cont.)*

Why Teach with a Roots Approach?

Teaching with a roots approach is efficient. Over 60 percent of the words students encounter in their reading have recognizable word parts (Nagy et al. 1989). Moreover, content-area vocabulary is largely of Greek and Latin origin (Harmon et al. 2005). Many words from Greek and Latin roots meet the criteria for "tier two" words and are appropriate for instruction (Beck, McKeown, and Kucan 2002).

Root study promotes independent word learning, even in the primary grades (Carlisle 2010). In addition, roots are word multipliers—that is, knowledge of one root can help students determine the meaning, pronunciation, and spelling of 10, 20, or more English words. With roots, students learn to make connections among words that are semantically related (Nagy and Scott 2000). Research suggests that the brain is a pattern detector (Cunningham 2004). Latin and Greek word roots follow linguistic patterns that can help students with the meaning, sound, and spelling of English words. Indeed, Latin and Greek roots have consistent orthographic (spelling) patterns (Rasinski and Padak 2013; Bear et al. 2011).

Latin and Greek word roots follow linguistic patterns that can help students with the meaning, sound, and spelling of English words.

Young readers' word instruction is often characterized by a study of word patterns called *rimes*, *phonograms*, or *word families*. A Latin-Greek roots approach is the next logical and developmental step in word learning (Bear et al. 2011). Many English language learners speak first languages semantically related to Latin. For example, more than 75 percent of the words in Spanish come from Latin (Chandler and Schwartz 1961/1991). In fact, Spanish, Portuguese, French, Catalan, Italian, and Rumanian are all classified as "Romance Languages" because they derive from Latin, the language of ancient Romans. Enhancing this natural linguistic connection inherent in many of these languages can accelerate these students' vocabulary growth (Blachowicz et al. 2006).

Many states are beginning to include a study of roots, including Latin and Greek derivations, in their elementary and middle school literacy standards. Indeed, the Common Core State Standards focus extensively on root-specific standards in the "Reading Foundational Skills" and "Language/ Vocabulary Acquisition and Use" sections. According to these standards, attention to roots should begin in kindergarten.

Vocabulary Research and Practice *(cont.)*

Differentiating Instruction

Some students, such as struggling readers or those learning English, may need additional support. Others may benefit from additional challenge. These ideas may help you differentiate instruction:

- Use visual aids.
- Ask students to sketch or act out words. Others can guess the depicted words.
- Reduce length of activity.
- Pair students. Encourage them to talk about the roots and the activities.
- Challenge students to create new words that contain the root. Others can guess what the made-up words mean.
- Talk students through the necessary process to complete an activity. Your aim should be to scaffold students' thinking, not to provide answers.
- As we point out in individual lesson descriptions, encourage talk.
- Have students keep a personal vocabulary journal in which they list the roots and related words they learn. Encourage students to use their new vocabulary in their oral and written language (e.g., "Use at least one word containing the *tract-* root in your journal entry today").
- Put the roots and words derived from the roots on display in the classroom. Keep them on display over the course of several weeks. (You may wish to move some of the displays into the hallway or other sites outside your classroom.)
- Play word games that involve the roots with your students often. Appendix E (pages 147–154) provides lists of words containing the roots used in this book.

Students who need additional challenge can a) look for words containing the featured root in their content-area texts, b) write riddles for others to solve using several words that contain the root, or c) use an online resource to find additional words containing the root (e.g., http://onelook.com) or to create word puzzles featuring the root (e.g., http://puzzlemaker.com).

Like their peers, English language learners benefit from the focus on meaning using research-based strategies to learn new roots and words. Especially if students' native languages derive from Latin (e.g., Spanish), make comparisons to the native languages whenever possible. (You can look online for resources to assist with this.) When Spanish speakers learn to look for roots within words, they will be able to relate many word roots in English to their counterparts in Spanish. Sharing their knowledge with other classmates will help everyone grow.

How to Use This Book

This book offers three units. Unit I presents three prefixes and two bases for words that appear in social studies. Unit II presents four prefixes and one base for words that appear in science. Unit III presents five numerical prefixes for words that appear in mathematics. The following information will help you implement each lesson within the three units.

Lesson Overview

A list of **Standards** (McREL and Common Core State Standards) is included in each lesson.

The **Materials** listed include the activity pages for students.

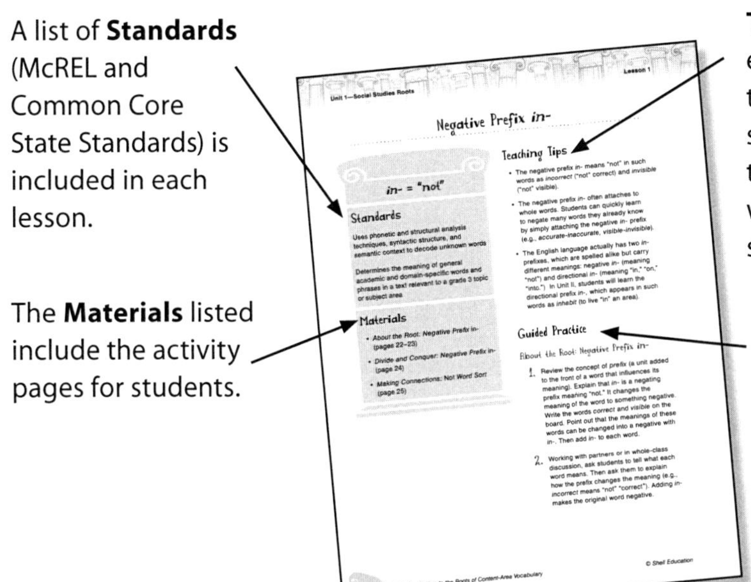

Unit 1—Social Studies Roots

Lesson 1

Negative Prefix *in-*

in- = "not"

Standards

Uses phonetic and structural analysis techniques, syntactic structure, and semantic context to decode unknown words

Determines the meaning of general academic and domain-specific words and phrases in a text relevant to a grade 3 topic or subject area

Materials

- *About the Root: Negative Prefix in-* (pages 22–23)
- *Divide and Conquer: Negative Prefix in-* (page 24)
- *Making Connections: Not Word Sort* (page 25)

Teaching Tips

- The negative prefix *in-* means "not" in such words as *incorrect* ("not" correct) and *invisible* ("not" visible).
- The negative prefix *in-* often attaches to whole words. Students can quickly learn to negate many words they already know by simply attaching the negative *in-* prefix (e.g., *accurate-inaccurate, visible-invisible*).
- The English language actually has two *in-* prefixes, which are spelled alike but carry different meanings: negative *in-* (meaning "not") and directional *in-* (meaning "in," "on," "into.") In Unit II, students will learn the directional prefix *in-*, which appears in such words as *inhabit* (to live "in" an area).

Guided Practice

About the Root: Negative Prefix *in-*

1. Review the concept of *prefix* (a unit added to the front of a word that influences its meaning). Explain that *in-* is a negating prefix meaning "not." It changes the meaning of the word to something negative. Write the words *correct* and *visible* on the board. Point out that the meanings of these words can be changed into a negative with *in-*. Then add *in-* to each word.
2. Working with partners or in whole-class discussion, ask students to tell what each word means. Then ask them to explain how the prefix changes the meaning (e.g., *incorrect* means "not" "correct"). Adding *in-* makes the original word negative.

20 #50863—Getting to the Roots of Content-Area Vocabulary © Shell Education

Teaching Tips provide essential information about the root. Reading this section before you teach the lesson will provide you with a foundation to ensure student success.

The **Guided Practice** portion of each lesson includes suggestions for implementing each of the student activity pages.

The **About the Root** activities are introductions and include short passages using the root of focus. The purpose of these passages is to show students contextual use of the root in the content areas. As students read to themselves or listen to the teacher read aloud, they identify the prefix or suffix words in extended texts that center on a wide range of interesting topics.

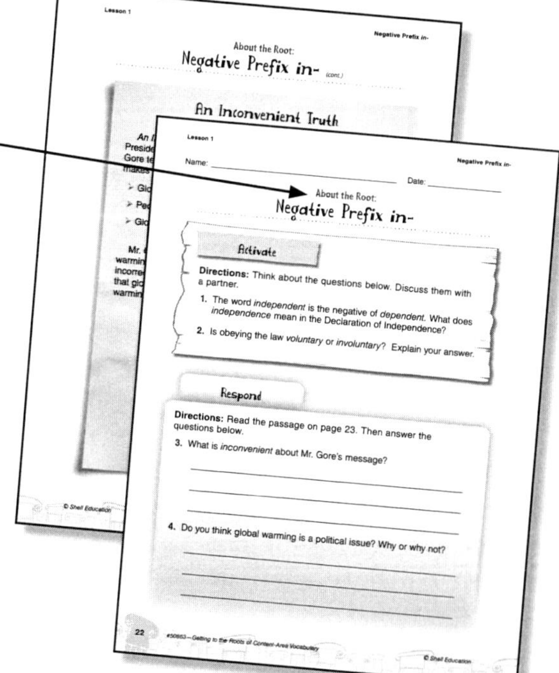

Lesson 1

Negative Prefix in-

About the Root:

Negative Prefix in- (cont.)

An Inconvenient Truth

© Shell Education

Lesson 1

Name: ______________________ Date: __________

Negative Prefix in-

About the Root:

Negative Prefix in-

Activate

Directions: Think about the questions below. Discuss them with a partner.

1. The word *independent* is the negative of *dependent*. What does *independence* mean in the Declaration of Independence?
2. Is obeying the law *voluntary* or *involuntary*? Explain your answer.

Respond

Directions: Read the passage on page 23. Then answer the questions below.

3. What is *inconvenient* about Mr. Gore's message?
4. Do you think global warming is a political issue? Why or why not?

22 #50863—Getting to the Roots of Content-Area Vocabulary © Shell Education

How to Use This Book *(cont.)*

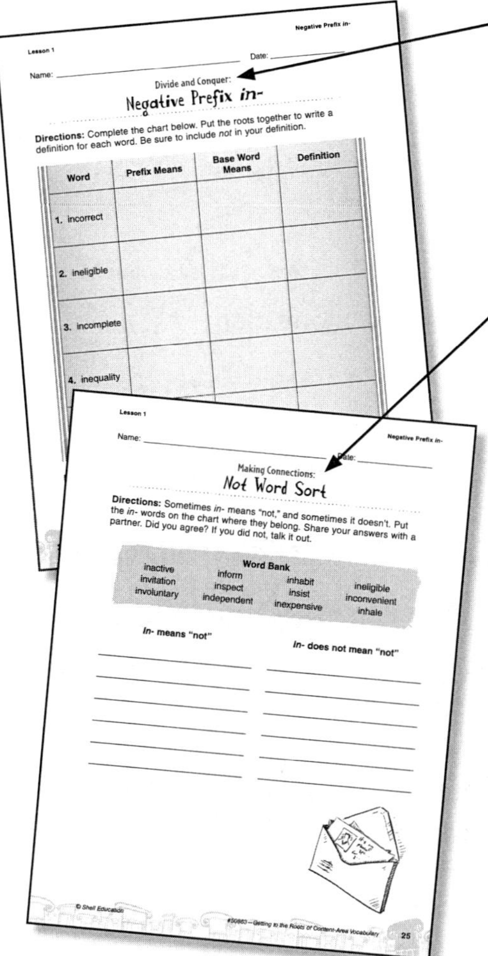

Lesson 1

Negative Prefix *in-*

Name: Date:

Divide and Conquer:

Negative Prefix *in-*

Directions: Complete the chart below. Put the roots together to write a definition for each word. Be sure to include *not* in your definition.

Word	Prefix Means	Base Word Means	Definition
1. incorrect			
2. ineligible			
3. incomplete			
4. inequality			

Lesson 1

Negative Prefix *in-*

Name: Date:

Making Connections:

Not Word Sort

Directions: Sometimes *in-* means "not," and sometimes it doesn't. Put the *in-* words on the chart where they belong. Share your answers with a partner. Did you agree? If you did not, talk it out.

Word Bank

inactive, invitation, involuntary, inform, inspect, independent, inhabit, insist, inexpensive, ineligible, inconvenient, inhale

In- means "not"	*In-* does not mean "not"

© Shell Education #50863—Getting to the Roots of Content-Area Vocabulary 25

The **Divide and Conquer** activities allow students to pull words apart. They dissect the parts of the words, understand the meaning of these parts, and then gain a greater understanding of the word as a whole.

The **Making Connections** activities allow students to use their knowledge of roots to make connections to vocabulary and offer students the opportunity to extend their exploration of the root(s) through activities such as word sorts, riddles, representing the roots and related words in drawings, and gamelike tasks. They may need to distinguish when to use a certain root or which way the root is used in a word.

All of the student activity pages and additional resources can be found in the **Digital Resources**.

How to Use This Book *(cont.)*

Tips for Implementation

These tips will help you think about how to teach the lessons in this book.

- You can teach the lessons in any order. You may want to coordinate with your curriculum and with your grade-level colleagues.
- Each lesson cycle addresses one root.
- Before beginning a new lesson, read the introductory information.
- Talking about the roots is very important for student learning. This approach to vocabulary development goes far beyond mere memorization of specific words (which, according to research, does not work). Students need to learn to think about how roots contribute to meanings. Talking this through can help them develop this realization. So, encourage students to talk, Talk, TALK!!! You will notice that the teacher directions for every Divide and Conquer activity include a brief etymological explanation of all words in the Divide and Conquer list. These explanations will help you guide the in-class discussion. These conversations, which need only take a few minutes, should focus on helping students think deeply about root meanings. For examples of etymological breakdown of the words, see the Answer Key (pages 115–121)

Note: We have suggested discussion questions and included answers for all of the Divide and Conquer activities. The answers are for your use only. They may help you lead discussions and conversations about how the roots contribute to meaning.

- Your direct involvement is needed for the Divide and Conquer activities. This is the process students use to determine meaning. They learn to look for meaningful chunks of words ("divide") and to use this information to "conquer" the meaning of the longer word. To help students see the logic inherent in divide and conquer, you can make an analogy to addition (*transport* = *trans* [across] + *port* [carry] = carry across) or "if/then" statements: If *trans* means "across" and *port* means "carry," then *transport* means…. "to carry something across an area." Be certain that students say the meaning of the longer word in a way that makes sense: "carry across," not "across carry." After students have divided and conquered, help them see how the roots "add up to" the meaning of the words.
- Students can complete the About the Root and Making Connections activities independently, in pairs, or as homework.
- Each week, display the root(s) and meaning(s) prominently in your classroom.

How to Use This Book *(cont.)*

- Encourage students to use the root of the week as much as possible. Reading, writing, speaking, and listening to words containing the root will facilitate learning. Several generic activities are suggested in Appendix C (pages 124–126) to provide additional instruction or practice, if you or your students wish.

Introducing Each Lesson

Introduce each root by linking to words that students already know. Ideas are provided in the Teaching Tips sections. In addition, you could:

- Put two or three common words containing the root on the board and ask students to talk about what meaning they share. You may want to embed these in phrases.
- Tell students, "The root of the week is ______. It means ______." Ask them to work with partners to generate words containing the root. Make a class list, and discuss common meaning.
- Encourage students to use the root's definition in their talk about words containing the root.

Assessment

At least one part of each lesson could be used for assessment purposes. In addition, you will find matching exercises that are suitable for assessment in Appendix D (pages 130–144) or in the Digital Resources (additionalassessments.pdf). You can use a simple three-point scale to record students' performances: Outstanding, Satisfactory, or Unsatisfactory. Informal assessment techniques can supplement this information:

- Use a knowledge-rating chart with students. To do this, select key words from something students will read. Make a three-column chart for students to indicate if they a) know a word well, b) have seen or heard it, or c) don't know it at all.
- Have students keep word journals in which they a) record information about roots and the words that contain them or b) keep lists of interesting words from their reading. Ask students to peruse their journals occasionally to draw some conclusions about their word knowledge.
- Encourage students to use self-assessment. Ask them to write about a) their own word knowledge, b) where they find new and interesting words, and/or c) what strategies they use most often to figure out the meaning of new words.

Correlation to the Standards

Shell Education is committed to producing educational materials that are research and standards based. In this effort, we have correlated all of our products to the academic standards of all 50 United States, the District of Columbia, the Department of Defense Dependent Schools, and all Canadian provinces.

How To Find Standards Correlations

To print a customized correlation report of this product for your state, visit our website at http://www.shelleducation.com and follow the on-screen directions. If you require assistance in printing correlation reports, please contact Customer Service at 1-877-777-3450.

Purpose and Intent of Standards

Legislation mandates that all states adopt academic standards that identify the skills students will learn in kindergarten through grade twelve. Many states also have standards for Pre–K. This same legislation sets requirements to ensure the standards are detailed and comprehensive.

Standards are designed to focus instruction and guide adoption of curricula. Standards are statements that describe the criteria necessary for students to meet specific academic goals. They define the knowledge, skills, and content students should acquire at each level. Standards are also used to develop standardized tests to evaluate students' academic progress. Teachers are required to demonstrate how their lessons meet state standards. State standards are used in the development of all of our products, so educators can be assured they meet the academic requirements of each state.

Common Core State Standards

Many lessons in this book are aligned to the Common Core State Standards (CCSS). The standards support the objectives presented throughout the lessons and are provided in the Digital Resources (standards.pdf).

McREL Compendium

We use the Mid-continent Research for Education and Learning (McREL) Compendium to create standards correlations. Each year, McREL analyzes state standards and revises the compendium. By following this procedure, McREL is able to produce a general compilation of national standards. Each lesson in this product is based on one or more McREL standards, which are provided in the Digital Resources (standards.pdf).

TESOL and WIDA Standards

The lessons in this book promote English language development for English language learners. The standards listed in the Digital Resources (standards.pdf) support the language objectives presented throughout the lessons.

Standards Chart

McREL Standard	Page(s)
Language Arts 5.4—Uses phonetic and structural analysis techniques, syntactic structure, and semantic context to decode unknown words	All Lessons
Language Arts 5.4—Uses a variety of context clues to decode unknown words	All Lessons
Common Core State Standard	**Page(s)**
Literacy.RI.3.4—Determine the meaning of general academic and domain-specific words and phrases in a text relevant to a grade 3 topic or subject area	All Lessons
Literacy.RF.3.3.a—Identify and know the meaning of the most common prefixes and derivational suffixes	All Lessons
Literacy.L.3.4.b—Determine the meaning of the new word formed when a known affix (or root) is added to a known word	All Lessons
Literacy.L.3.4.c—Use a known root word as a clue to the meaning of an unknown word with the same root	All Lessons
TESOL and WIDA Standard	**Page(s)**
English language learners **communicate** for **social**, **intercultural**, and **instructional** purposes within the school setting	All Lessons
English language learners **communicate** information, ideas, and concepts necessary for academic success in the area of **language arts**	All Lessons

About the Authors

Timothy Rasinski, Ph.D., is a professor of literacy education at Kent State University. He has written over 150 articles and has authored, coauthored, or edited over 15 books and curriculum programs on reading education. His research on reading has been cited by the National Reading Panel and has been published in journals such as *Reading Research Quarterly, The Reading Teacher, Reading Psychology*, and *The Journal of Educational Research.* Tim served on the Board of Directors of the International Reading Association, and from 1992–1999, he was coeditor of *The Reading Teacher*, the world's most widely read journal of literacy education. He has also served as editor of the *Journal of Literacy Research*, one of the premier research journals in reading. Tim is a past president of the College Reading Association, and he has won the A.B. Herr Award from the College Reading Association for his scholarly contributions to literacy education. In 2010, Tim was elected into the International Reading Hall of Fame.

Nancy Padak, Ed.D., is an active researcher, author, and consultant. She was a Distinguished Professor in the College and Graduate School of Education, Health, and Human Services at Kent State University. She directed KSU's Reading and Writing Center and taught in the area of literacy education. She was the Principal Investigator for the Ohio Literacy Resource Center, which has provided support for adult and family literacy programs since 1993. Prior to her arrival at Kent State in 1985, she was a classroom teacher and district administrator. She has written or edited more than 25 books and more than 90 chapters and articles. She has also served in a variety of leadership roles in professional organizations, including the presidency of the College Reading Association and (with others) the Editor of *The Reading Teacher* and the *Journal of Literacy Research.* She has won several awards for her scholarship and contributions to literacy education.

About the Authors *(cont.)*

Rick M. Newton, Ph.D., holds a doctoral degree in Greek and Latin from the University of Michigan and is now an emeritus professor of Greek and Latin at Kent State University. He developed the course "English Words from Classical Elements," which more than 15,000 Kent State students have taken over the past 30 years. He holds the Distinguished Teaching Award from the Kent State College of Arts and Sciences and the Translation Award from the Modern Greek Studies Association of North America and Canada.

Evangeline Newton, Ph.D., is a professor of literacy education at the University of Akron, where she served as the first director of the Center for Literacy. She teaches a variety of literacy methods courses and professional development workshops to elementary, middle, and high school teachers. A former coeditor of *The Ohio Reading Teacher*, Evangeline currently chairs the Reading Review Board of the Ohio Resource Center for Mathematics, Science, and Reading. She serves on editorial review boards for *The Reading Teacher* and *Reading Horizons*. Evangeline is active in the Association of Literacy Educators and the International Reading Association (IRA). As a participant in IRA's Reading and Writing for Critical Thinking project, Evangeline taught workshops for teachers and Peace Corps volunteers in Armenia. A former St. Louis public school teacher, Evangeline holds a B.A. from Washington University in St. Louis, an M.A.T. from Webster University, and a Ph.D. from Kent State University.

Negative Prefix *in-*

***in-* = "not"**

Standards

Uses phonetic and structural analysis techniques, syntactic structure, and semantic context to decode unknown words

Determines the meaning of general academic and domain-specific words and phrases in a text relevant to a grade 3 topic or subject area

Materials

- *About the Root: Negative Prefix* in- (pages 22–23)
- *Divide and Conquer: Negative Prefix* in- (page 24)
- *Making Connections:* Not *Word Sort* (page 25)

Teaching Tips

- The negative prefix *in-* means "not" in such words as *incorrect* ("not" correct) and *invisible* ("not" visible).
- The negative prefix *in-* often attaches to whole words. Students can quickly learn to negate many words they already know by simply attaching the negative *in-* prefix (e.g., *accurate-inaccurate, visible-invisible*).
- The English language actually has two *in-* prefixes, which are spelled alike but carry different meanings: negative *in-* (meaning "not") and directional *in-* (meaning "in," "on," "into.") In Unit II, students will learn the directional prefix *in-,* which appears in such words as *inhabit* (to live "in" an area).

Guided Practice

About the Root: Negative Prefix *in-*

1. Review the concept of *prefix* (a unit added to the front of a word that influences its meaning). Explain that *in-* is a negating prefix meaning "not." It changes the meaning of the word to something negative. Write the words *correct* and *visible* on the board. Point out that the meanings of these words can be changed into a negative with *in-*. Then add *in-* to each word.
2. Working with partners or in whole-class discussion, ask students to tell what each word means. Then ask them to explain how the prefix changes the meaning (e.g., *incorrect* means "not" "correct"). Adding *in-* makes the original word negative.

Negative Prefix *in-* (cont.)

3. Write the word *eligible* on the board. Ask students to list groups of people who are eligible to vote in United States' elections. Now add the prefix *in-* to *eligible* and ask students to list groups of people who are ineligible to vote. Draw students' attention to how the addition of the prefix *in-* changed the meaning of *eligible* from positive (can vote) to negative (cannot vote).

4. Tell students that *in-* does not always mean "not." Remind them to consider the meaning and context of a word when determining if *in-* means "not." Ask students if such words as *include* or *inhabit* begin with negative *in-*. Point out that since these words have no negative meaning, they do not begin with negative *in-*. Have continued discussions about word meanings to build students' word-analysis skill, as well as build their capacity to use context clues.

5. After students have discussed the Activate questions, invite whole-group conversation. You may wish to have students write down the shared ideas to revisit at a later time.

Divide and Conquer: Negative Prefix *in-*

6. As you guide students through Divide and Conquer, use the questions below to generate discussion about each of the words:

- Where is the meaning of "not" in the word ______?
- Where might you see the word ______?
- Can you think of an example of ______?
- Does ______ have more than one meaning? If so, how are those meanings the same? How are they different?
- How is the word ______ different from the word ______?

  Note: The suffix *-ible* means "ability," or "capacity," and the suffix *-ity* means "quality of being." Help students see how the suffixes contribute to meaning.

Making Connections: Not Word Sort

7. Have students work with partners. Have them discuss words that they had a hard time categorizing. You may also have them write sentences using negative *in-* words and share them with others.

Words with *in-* (negative)

inaccurate	indirect
inactive	indisputable
inadmissible	indivisible
inalienable	ineffective
inappropriate	ineligible
incapable	inexact
incompetent	inexcusable
incomplete	inexpensive
inconclusive	inhumane
inconvenient	inoffensive
incorrect	insufficient
indecent	intolerant
indefensible	invalid
independence	invisible
independent	involuntary

To print a full list of words for students, see page 147.

Name: ______________________________ Date: ________________

About the Root:

Negative Prefix *in-*

Activate

Directions: Think about the questions below. Discuss them with a partner.

1. The word *independent* is the negative of *dependent.* What does *independence* mean in the Declaration of Independence?

2. Is obeying the law *voluntary* or *involuntary*? Explain your answer.

Respond

Directions: Read the passage on page 23. Then answer the questions below.

3. What is *inconvenient* about Mr. Gore's message?

____

____

____

4. Do you think global warming is a political issue? Why or why not?

____

____

____

About the Root:
Negative Prefix *in-* (cont.)

An Inconvenient Truth

An Inconvenient Truth is the name of a 2006 movie. Former Vice President Al Gore is the main person in the movie. In the movie, Mr. Gore teaches people about climate change and global warming. He makes three big points:

- Global warming is real.
- People cause global warming.
- Global warming will lead to terrible problems.

Mr. Gore wants people to take action to slow or stop global warming. Some people do this. Others think that Mr. Gore is incorrect; he was just playing politics. Some people do not believe that global warming is real. They feel that the research about global warming is incomplete.

Name: ______________________________ Date: ______________

Divide and Conquer:
Negative Prefix *in-*

Directions: Complete the chart below. Put the roots together to make a definition for each word. Be sure to include *not* in your definition. Then complete the activity.

Word	Prefix Means	Base Means	Definition
1. incorrect			
2. ineligible			
3. incomplete			
4. inequality			
5. incredible			

6. Work with a partner. Explain how the words above include the idea of "not."

Name: ______________________________ Date: ______________

Making Connections:

Not Word Sort

Directions: Sometimes *in-* means "not," and sometimes it doesn't. Put the *in-* words on the chart where they belong. Share your answers with a partner. Did you agree? If you did not, talk it out.

Word Bank

inactive	inform	inhabit	ineligible
invitation	inspect	insist	inconvenient
involuntary	independent	inexpensive	inhale

***In-* means "not"**	***In-* does not mean "not"**
______________	______________
______________	______________
______________	______________
______________	______________
______________	______________
______________	______________

Prefix *co-, con-*

co-, con- = "with," "together"

Standards

Uses phonetic and structural analysis techniques, syntactic structure, and semantic context to decode unknown words

Determines the meaning of the new word formed when a known root is added to a known word

Materials

- *About the Root: Prefix co-, con-* (pages 28–29)
- *Divide and Conquer: Prefix co-, con-* (page 30)
- *Making Connections: Draw It!* (page 31)

Teaching Tips

The prefix co-, con- means "with" or "together." These prefixes attach to whole words and to bases that are not whole words. In general, *co-* attaches to whole words (e.g., *cooperate, coworker, coauthor, cosponsor*) and *con-* attaches to bases (e.g., *congress, contract*).

Guided Practice

About the Root: Prefix *co-, con-*

1. Invite two students to come to the front of the room and act out the concept of cooperating with each other (e.g., students may demonstrate working together helping each other). Ask students what they do when they cooperate with each other. Draw their attention to the idea that they work "together."

2. Write the word *cooperate* on the board. Draw a line between the prefix *co-* and the base *operate*. Tell students that *co-* and *con-* are prefixes that mean "with" or "together." The base *oper-* means "work." Therefore, *co* + *operate* = "work together."

3. Write the word *congregate* on the board. Ask students to talk with partners about what this word means and how it incorporates the idea of "with" or "together." In the course of discussion, explain that the base *greg-* means "flock" or "herd." Therefore, *con* + *gregate* = "flock together."

4. After students have discussed the Activate questions, invite whole-group conversation. You may wish to have students write down the shared ideas to revisit at a later time.

Prefix co-, con- *(cont.)*

Divide and Conquer: Prefix co-, con-

5. As you guide students through Divide and Conquer, use the questions below to generate discussion about each of the words:

   - Where is the meaning of "with" or "together" in the word ______?
   - Where might you see the word ______?
   - Can you think of an example of ______?
   - Does ______ have more than one meaning? If so, how are those meanings the same? How are they different?
   - How is the word ______ different from the word ______?

   Note: The suffix *-ate* makes a word on the chart a verb. The suffix *-ion* means "condition" or "action." Help students see how the suffixes contribute to meaning.

Making Connections: Draw It!

6. Discuss the word *codefendant* to students prior to implementing the activity.

7. As a follow-up, small groups of students can act out one of the situations. Have other students guess which situation is portrayed.

Words with co- and con-

coalition	conspiring
coauthor	conspired
coexist	conspirator
cohabitate	constituent
confederate	continent
conference	convention
conflict	cooperate
congress	cooperated
conflict	cooperating
conservation	cooperation
conspire	coworker
conspiracy	

To print a full list of words for students, see page 147.

Name: ________________________________ Date: ______________

About the Root:

Prefix *co-*, *con-*

Activate

Directions: Think about the questions below. Discuss them with a partner.

1. How does *coworker* include the idea of "with" or "together"?

2. Fill in the blanks with *co-* words: Who are we?

   - We fly a plane together. We are ____________________.
   - We wrote a book together. We are ____________________.

Respond

Directions: Read the passage on page 29. Then answer the question below.

3. The prefix *con-* means "with" or "together." The base *gress-* means "step." Explain how this prefix and base go together to make the word *congress*.

____

____

____

____

____

____

About the Root:

Prefix co-, con- (cont.)

Understanding Congress

The word *congress* can describe lots of groups. But we usually think of Congress as the law-making body of the United States government. Congress has 535 elected members. One hundred are Senators, and 435 are members of the House of Representatives. In the United States Congress, hundreds of legislators must work together for the common good. It is not uncommon for two or more members of Congress to get together and co-sponsor a bill with one another.

Congress can also refer to a meeting of this group. For example, the 113th Congress began in January 2013. Since House members are elected every two years, the people in Congress change every two years. This is why each Congress meets for two years. Members of Congress cooperate with the president to make laws for the country.

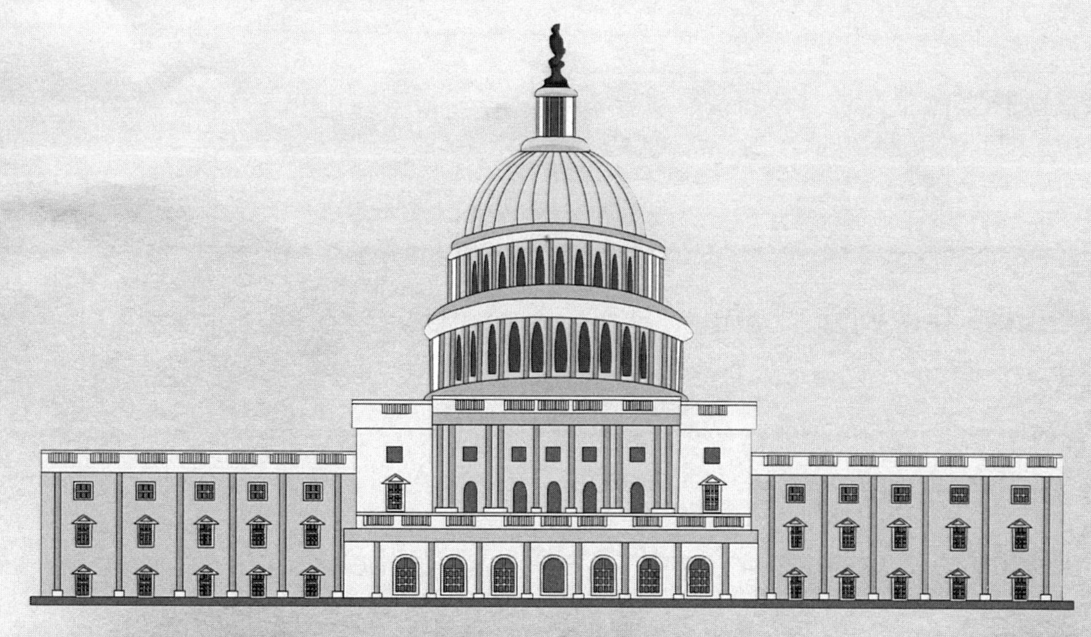

Name: ______________________________ Date: ______________

Divide and Conquer:
Prefix *co-*, *con-*

Directions: Complete the chart below. Put the roots together to make a definition for each word. Be sure to use *with* or *together* in your definition.

Word	Prefix Means	Base Means	Definition
1. coauthor			
2. cooperate			
3. contract		*tract* = pull, draw, drag	
4. congregation		*greg-* = flock, herd	
5. construct		*struct-* = build	

Directions: Talk with a partner. Write your answers on a separate sheet of paper.

6. Do *coauthors* need to *cooperate*? Explain.
7. Describe *construction* using "with" or "together."
8. Explain to a partner how a *contraction* includes the idea of "with" or "together."

Name: ______________________________ Date: ______________

Making Connections:
Draw It!

Directions: Choose two situations listed below. Make a drawing that shows what each one means. Then trade papers with a partner. See if your partner can figure out the situations you used.

Situations

- two children playing *cooperatively*
- a meeting of *Congress*
- the *conductor* of an orchestra
- *codefendants* at a trial
- *coworkers constructing* a building

Prefixes *com-* and *col-*

com-, col- = "with," "together"

Standards

Uses a variety of context clues to decode unknown words

Identifies and knows the meaning of the most common prefixes and derivational suffixes

Materials

- *About the Root: Prefixes* com- *and* col- (pages 34–35)
- *Divide and Conquer: Prefixes* com- *and* col- (page 36)
- *Making Connections:* con- *or* com-? (page 37)

Teaching Tips

- *Com-* and *col-* are Latin prefixes meaning "with" or "together." They are forms of the Latin prefix *con-* that have undergone assimilation. For more information on assimilation, see pages 8–9.
- The prefix *con-* assimilates into *com-* when the next letter in the word is an *m* or a *p*. Words like *combine* (not *conbine*) and *compose* (not *conpose*) are clear examples. Notice how difficult it would be to pronounce the unassimilated words *conbine* and *conpose*.
- The prefix *con-* assimilates into *col-* when the next letter in the word is an *l*. Words like *collide* (not *conlide*) and *collect* (not *conlect*) are clear examples. Again, notice how difficult it would be to pronounce the unassimilated words *conlide* and *conlect*.

Guided Practice

About the Root: Prefixes *com-* and *col-*

1. Write the words *community* and *collision* on the board. Tell students that it may not look like it, but each of these words contains the *con-* prefix. Draw lines after *com-* and *col-*. Now write *connunity* under *community* and *conlision* under *collision*. Ask students to turn to a neighbor and say each set of words. Guide them to understand that the *com-* and *col-* words are easier to pronounce. Explain that many words beginning with *com-* or *col-* have "with" or "together" in their meanings, just as words beginning with *co-* and *con-* do. Finally, ask pairs of students to talk about *community* and *collision*. Where is the "with" or "together" in their meanings?

Prefixes *com-* and *col-* (cont.)

2. Ask students to complete the About the Root pages. They can work individually or with partners. After they have finished, invite whole-group conversation. Students can share answers, talk about the text passage, or generate more words containing the root.

3. After students have discussed the Activate questions, invite whole-group conversation. You may wish to have students write down the shared ideas to revisit at a later time.

Divide and Conquer: Prefixes *com-* and *col-*

4. As you guide students through Divide and Conquer, use the questions below to generate discussion about each of the words:

   - Where is the meaning of "with" or "together" in the word ______?
   - Where might you see the word ______?
   - Can you think of an example of ______?
   - Does ______ have more than one meaning? If so, how are those meanings the same? How are they different?
   - How is the word ______ different from the word ______?

   Note: The suffix *-ion* means "state," "condition," or "action." Help students see how the suffix contributes to meaning.

Making Connections: *con-* or *com-*?

5. Students can complete the Word Sort alone or with partners.

6. Invite sharing once students have completed their work.

Words with *com-* and *col-*

collaborate	commonwealth
collateral	commune
collect	communal
collected	communicate
collecting	communicated
collective	communicating
collector	communicator
college	communism
collegian	community
collegiate	compact
combine	compromise
combination	compromised
common	compromising
commoner	

To print a full list of words for students, see page 148.

Name: ______________________________ Date: ______________

About the Root:

Prefixes *com-* and *col-*

Activate

Directions: Think about how to make new words using the *col-* and *com-* words below. Discuss them with a partner.

1. someone who **col**lects
2. a group of things that have been **col**lected
3. someone who **com**poses
4. something that has been **com**posed

Respond

Directions: Read the passage on page 35. Then answer the question below.

5. Pick one community. Explain what values members of this group share.

____

____

____

____

____

____

____

About the Root:
Prefixes *com-* and *col-* *(cont.)*

Communities

You are part of a community. In fact, you may be part of more than one community. A *community* is a group that shares values. So your town or city is a community, and you are a community member. You are also part of your school community. You may also be part of a religious community. In each case—town, school, or religious group—community members share collective values. They work collectively for the betterment of their group.

Are you part of any groups on the Internet? For example, do you follow sports teams or entertainers online? If so, this makes you a part of a virtual community.

Name: ________________________ Date: ______________

Divide and Conquer:
Prefixes *com-* and *col-*

Directions: Complete the chart below. Put the roots together to make a definition for each word. Be sure to use *with* or *together* in your definition.

Word	Prefix Means	Base Means	Definition
1. collide		*lid-* = strike, crash	
2. compose		*pos-* = put, place	
3. collection		*lect-* = choose, gather	
4. compete		*pet-* = seek, pursue	
5. compress		*press-* = press, squeeze	

6. Work with a partner. Write a sentence using at least two words from the chart.

____

____

Name: ______________________________ Date: ______________

Making Connections:
con- or com-?

Directions: Work with a partner to put the word parts on the chart where they belong. Some words begin with *con-*, and others begin with *com-*. Write the complete word.

Word Bank

centrate	pile	struct	duct
pact	coct	panion	ference
mune	fer	press	bine

con-	***com-***
______________	______________
______________	______________
______________	______________
______________	______________
______________	______________
______________	______________

Look at the spellings of the words in each column. Work with a partner to make a rule for when you should use *con-* and when you should use *com-*.

____

____

____

____

Base *port-*

port- = "carry"

Standards

Uses a variety of context clues to decode unknown words

Uses a known root word as a clue to the meaning of an unknown word with the same root

Materials

- *About the Root: Base* port- (pages 40–41)
- *Divide and Conquer: Base* port- (page 42)
- *Making Connections: Riddle Me This* (page 43)

Teaching Tips

The first three lessons in this unit have presented prefixes. This lesson introduces a base. You may wish to review with your students the difference between a prefix and a base. *Prefixes* appear at the beginnings of words, and they influence basic meaning (e.g., by negating or providing direction). *Bases* are roots that give words their basic core meanings. The Latin base *port-* means "carry."

Guided Practice

About the Root: Base *port-*

1. Ask students what a cell phone, a laptop, and a suitcase have in common. Point out that all three items can be carried. Now write the word *portable* on the board. Underline *port*, and explain that *port* means "to carry." Ask students to talk with a partner to define *portable* using the word *carry*.

2. Have students complete the About the Root pages. They can work individually or with partners. After they have finished, invite whole-group conversation. Students can share answers, talk about the text passage, or generate more words containing the root.

3. After students have discussed the Activate questions, invite whole-group conversation. You may wish to have students write down the shared ideas to revisit at a later time.

Base *port-* (cont.)

Divide and Conquer: Base *port-*

4. As you guide students through Divide and Conquer, use the questions below to generate discussion about each of the words:

   - Where is the meaning of "carry" in the word ______?
   - Where might you see the word ______?
   - Can you think of an example of ______?
   - Does ______ have more than one meaning? If so, how are those meanings the same? How are they different?
   - How is the word ______ different from the word ______?

   Note: The suffix *-er* means "one who," and the suffix *-able* means "able." Help students understand how the suffixes contribute to meaning.

Making Connections: Riddle Me This

5. Have students complete the parts of this activity alone or with partners.

6. Provide time for students to share and discuss their riddles.

Words with *port-*

airport	importation
comport	importer
deport	imported
deportation	port
deported	portage
deporting	porter
export	report
exported	reported
exporting	reporter
exporter	reporting
import	reports

To print a full list of words for students, see page 148.

Name: ______________________________ Date: ______________

About the Root:
Base *port-*

Activate

Directions: Think about the questions below. Discuss them with a partner.

1. If *-port-* means "carry" and *trans-* means "across," what does *transport* mean?
2. If *ex-* means "out," what does *export* mean?

Respond

Directions: Read the passage on page 41. Then answer the question below.

3. Talk with a partner. Why do you think importing and exporting are important for our country?

____

____

____

____

____

____

____

About the Root:
Base port- *(cont.)*

Exports and Imports

The Port of New Orleans is one of the largest transportation hubs in the United States. It is located near the lower Mississippi River. Railroads and interstate highway systems are connected to the port. Here, we import such things as bananas, rubber, and coffee from South America. We also export steel and other manufactured goods made in the United States to other countries. For example, more than half the nation's grain exports leave the country through the Port of New Orleans. Both importing and exporting are important for our country.

Name: ______________________________ Date: ________________

Divide and Conquer:
Base *port-*

Directions: Complete the chart below. An *X* means that the word has no prefix. Put the roots together to make a definition for each word. Be sure to use *carry* in your definition.

Word	Prefix Means	Base Means	Definition
1. export	*ex-* = out		
2. transport	*trans-* = across, change		
3. porter	X		
4. portage	X		
5. deport	*de-* = down, off of		

Directions: Talk about the question below with a partner.

6. How are *export* and *transport* the same? How are they different?

____

____

____

Name: ______________________________ Date: ________________

Making Connections:
Riddle Me This

Directions: Answer the riddles. All answers will have *port-* in them. Then create your own riddle.

1. I am a person.

My job is to carry things.

I might work on a train or in a hotel.

Who am I?

____

2. You might have me in your classroom.

I would be a place to keep the papers you want to save and keep flat.

(**Hint**: "Papers" can be called "folios" because they are flat like leaves.)

If you wanted to, you could carry me to your desk or take me home.

I have four syllables.

What am I?

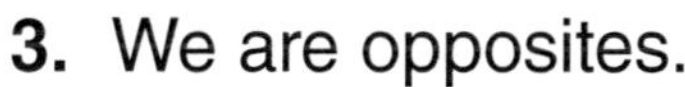

3. We are opposites.

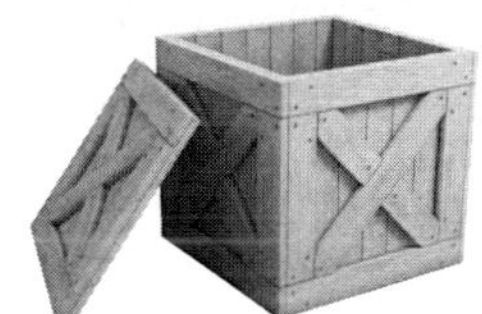

One of us means "carry in."

One of us means "carry out."

We describe goods and services that countries sell or buy.

Each of us has two syllables.

What are we?

______________________________ ______________________________

4. Choose one of the following words: *portable*, *transportation*, *airport*, or *deport*. Write your own riddle on a separate sheet of paper. Ask your partner to solve the riddle.

Bases *mov-*, *mot-*, and *mobil-*

mov-, *mot-*, *mobil-* = "move"

Standards

Uses phonetic and structural analysis techniques, syntactic structure, and semantic context to decode unknown words

Determines the meaning of general academic and domain-specific words and phrases in a text relevant to a grade 3 topic or subject area

Materials

- *About the Root: Bases* mov-, mot-, *and* mobil- (pages 46–47)
- *Divide and Conquer: Bases* mov-, mot-, *and* mobil- (page 48)
- *Making Connections: Moving or Not Moving?* (page 49)

Teaching Tips

The Latin bases *mov-, mot-,* and *mobil-* mean "move." The three forms of this base (*mov-, mot-, mobil-*) are identical in meaning. Words with this base are usually active and lively. Many "motion" words (e.g., *automobile, motor, locomotive, movie)* are already familiar to students.

Guided Practice

About the Root: Bases *mov-*, *mot-*, and *mobil-*

1. Ask students to:
   - put their hands on their heads. Then *remove* them.
   - *motion* "bye-bye" with their hands.
   - pretend to drive an *automobile*.
2. Write *remove*, *motion*, and *automobile* on the board. Underline *mov-*, *mot-*, and *mobil*. Ask students to talk to partners about what these roots mean. Accept predictions. Then tell students that *mov-*, *mot-* and *mobil-* are all forms of the same base, which means "move."
3. Ask students to complete the About the Root pages. They can work individually or with partners. After they have finished, invite whole-group conversation. Students can share answers, talk about the text passage, or generate more words containing the root.
4. After students have discussed the Activate questions, invite whole-group conversation. You may wish to have students write down the shared ideas to revisit at a later time.

Bases *mov-*, *mot-*, and *mobil-* *(cont.)*

Divide and Conquer: Bases *mov-*, *mot-*, and *mobil-*

5. As you guide students through Divide and Conquer, use the questions below to generate discussion about each of the words:

- Where is the meaning of "move" in the word ______?
- Where might you see the word ______?
- Can you think of an example of ______?
- Does ______ have more than one meaning? If so, how are those meanings the same? How are they different?
- How is the word ______ different from the word ______?

Note: The suffix *-ion* means "state," "condition," or "action." Help students see how the suffix contributes to meaning.

Making Connections: Moving or Not Moving?

6. Have students complete the activity with partners.

7. To conclude this activity, invite sharing. Ask students to explain their reasons for sorting words as they did. Emphasize the "move" in each word.

Words with *mov-*, *mot-*, and *mobil-*

automobile	motorize
commotion	move
immobile	moved
locomotive	mover
locomotion	moving
mobilize	movement
mobilization	promote
mobility	promoted
motion	promoter
motivate	promoting
motivated	promotion
motivating	remove
motivator	removal
motive	removed
motor	removing

To print a full list of words for students, see page 149.

Name: ______________________ Date: ______________

About the Root:

Bases *mov-*, *mot-*, and *mobil-*

Activate

Directions: Talk with a partner. Where is the "move" in each of the words below?

1. bookmobile ______________________
2. commotion ______________________
3. motorboat ______________________

Respond

Directions: Read the passage on page 47. Then answer the question below.

4. The Interstate highway system affected travel. How do you think it affected transportation?

____
____
____
____
____
____
____

About the Root:

Bases *mov-*, *mot-*, and *mobil-* (cont.)

Motels

Motel is a blended word. It is a shortened form of *motor* and *hotel*. If you think about the meaning of these two words, you can figure out what motels are.

Beginning in the 1920s, highways were built across America. In the 1950s, President Eisenhower led the development of the interstate highway system. Now people could travel by automobile. They needed roadside hotels in which to spend the night during their travels.

These roadside hotels were usually single buildings, and rooms were connected to each other. Doors opened onto parking lots. These "motor hotels" became known as *motels* because they were designed for people on the move.

Name: ______________________________ Date: ______________

Divide and Conquer:

Bases *mov-*, *mot-*, and *mobil-*

Directions: Complete the chart below. An *X* means that the word has no prefix. Put the roots together to make a definition for each word. Be sure to use *move* in your definition.

Word	Prefix Means	Base Means	Definition
1. promote	*pro-* = forward, ahead		
2. commotion	*com-* = with, together		
3. mobile	X		
4. motion	X		
5. remove	*re-* = back, again		

Directions: Talk with a partner to answer the questions below. Write your answers on a separate sheet of paper.

6. Which kind of house would be easier to move—a *mobile* home or an *immobile* home? Why?
7. Could a *promotion* cause a *commotion*? Explain.

Name: ______________________________ Date: ______________

Making Connections:

Moving or Not Moving?

Directions: All of the words in the Word Bank begin with *mot-*. Some have something to do with moving, and some do not. Put the words in the correct column on the chart.

Word Bank

mote	mother	motivate	motorized
motel	motion	motorist	motto

Has to do with moving	Does not have to do with moving
____________	____________
____________	____________
____________	____________
____________	____________
____________	____________
____________	____________

Directions: Write sentences for three of the words that have something to do with moving. Leave blanks where the words belong. Then trade papers with a partner. Ask your partner to fill in the blanks.

____

____

____

Name: ______________________________ Date: ______________

Unit I Review:
Social Studies Crossword Puzzle

Directions: Use words from the Word Bank and the clues below to complete the crossword puzzle on page 51.

Word Bank

coauthors	compose	deport	incorrect
collect	Congress	export	indivisible
collide	cooperate	import	involuntary
compete	coworker	incomplete	transport

Across

1. This year, the United States will again ______ many goods from China.
2. During elections, candidates may ______ on several important issues.
3. We now have a voluntary military, but once military service was ______.
6. Each year the Internal Revenue Service will ______ taxes.
9. The United Nations hopes that countries will ______ to solve problems.
10. A ______ is someone who works alongside someone else.
12. How many ______ were there for the Constitution?
13. Republicans and Democrats ______ against each other in most elections.

Down

1. "One nation under God, ______" means that our nation cannot be divided.
4. When someone runs for reelection, he or she often says, "I need more time because my plans are ______."
5. The United States may ______ persons who are in the country illegally.
6. The United States ______ includes the House of Representatives and the Senate.
7. Ships, trains, and trucks are used to ______ goods from one place to another.
8. Some people believe that the Supreme Court can make an ______ decision.
11. Do we import more goods and products than we ______?
12. Groups of Representatives and Senators often get together to ______ new laws.

Name: ______________________________ Date: ________________

Unit I Review:
Social Studies Crossword Puzzle (cont.)

Directions: Use the words from the Word Bank and the clues on page 50 to complete the crossword puzzle below.

Prefixes e- and ex-

e-, ex- = "out"

Standards

Uses a variety of context clues to decode unknown words

Identifies and knows the meaning of the most common prefixes and derivational suffixes

Materials

- *About the Root: Prefixes* e- *and* ex- (pages 54–55)
- *Divide and Conquer: Prefixes* e- *and* ex- (page 56)
- *Making Connections: Guess My Picture!* (page 57)

Teaching Tips

- The prefixes *e-* and *ex-* mean "out" and can attach to both whole words and Latin bases. This lesson focuses on familiar school words in which *e-* or *ex-* attaches to bases. For example, an *explosion* is an outburst; when a volcano *erupts,* flames and gases burst out of the mountain; rushing water *erodes* soil by washing it out, resulting in *erosion.*
- Ease of pronunciation determines whether *e-* or *ex-* is used. For example, we can easily pronounce such words as *exclude* ("to shut out"), *excavate* ("to dig or hollow out"), *exhaust* ("to drain out"), *expand* ("to spread out") and *expose* ("to put out, as to put out in the light or to put out in harm's way"). But because we cannot easily pronounce such words as *exrupt* or *exrode*, the *x* has been dropped: *erupt, erode.*
- When attached to intact words with a dash, the prefix *ex-* usually means "former" (e.g., *ex-employer, ex-friend, ex-spouse*).

Guided Practice

About the Root: Prefixes e- and ex-

1. Review the concept of prefix (unit added to the front of a word that influences its meaning; many prefixes are directional in force). Write the word *exit* on the board. Ask a student to exit the room and then come back. Ask the class where the student went when he or she exited the room. Draw their attention to the idea that he or she went out of the room. Tell students that *ex-* is a prefix meaning "out." The Latin base *it-* means "go." Thus, when we exit a room, we "go out" of it.

Prefixes e- and ex- *(cont.)*

2. Write the word *exhale* on the board. Ask students to exhale. Where did their breath go when they exhaled? (It went out of their bodies.) Put a slash between *ex-* and *hale*. Explain that *hale* is a Latin base that means "breathe." Remind them that the base (*hale*) carries the main meaning, so *exhale* means to "breathe out." Ask them to fill in these blanks as you read this sentence aloud: If *hale* means ______, and *ex-* means ______, then *exhale* means ______.

3. Write the word *evacuate* on the board. Tell students that the Latin base *vacu-* means "empty." Ask students to share a sentence like the one that you made for *exhale*. Explain that the prefixes *e-* and *ex-* mean "out."

4. Ask students to complete the About the Root pages. They can work individually or with partners. After they have finished, invite whole-group conversation. Students can share answers, talk about the text passage, or generate more words containing the root.

5. After students have discussed the Activate questions, invite whole-group conversation. You may wish to have students write down the shared ideas to revisit at a later time.

Divide and Conquer: Prefixes e- and ex-

6. As you guide students through Divide and Conquer, use the questions below to generate discussion about each of the words:

- Where is the meaning of "out" in the word ______?
- Where might you see the word ______?
- Can you think of an example of ______?
- Does ______ have more than one meaning? If so, how are those meanings the same? How are they different?
- How is the word ______ different from the word ______?

Making Connections: Guess My Picture!

7. To conclude this activity, ask students to tell where the "out" is in each word.

Words with e- and ex-

exact	expend
exacted	expended
exacting	expending
examine	experiment
excavate	expire
excision	expired
excursion	expiring
exert	expiration
exfoliate	explode
exhale	explosion
exhaust	exploding
exhume	exploded
exist	explore
exit	expose
expand	extinct
expanded	extrude
expanding	extrusion
expansion	extruder
expel	extruding
expelling	extruded
expelled	

To print a full list of words for students, see page 149.

Name: ______________________ Date: ______________

About the Root:

Prefixes e- and ex-

Activate

Directions: Answer the questions below. Discuss them with a partner.

1. Do you *exhale* when you sneeze? Explain your answer.
2. The vet *excised* a growth from our dog's leg. What did the vet do? (**Hint**: The base *cis*- means "cut.")

Respond

Directions: Read the passage on page 55. Then answer the question below.

3. The word *experiment* is related to the word *experience*. Both words have two roots—*ex*- means "out," and *peritus*- means "test" or "try." Explain how the meanings of *experiment* and *experience* are connected.

____

____

____

____

____

About the Root:

Prefixes *e-* and *ex-* *(cont.)*

Let's Experiment!

The purpose of an experiment is to try something "out." This is why the word begins with the prefix *ex-*. We all know that scientists do experiments to try out new ideas. But did you know that children and babies experiment, too? Experiments can be loose and informal or highly controlled. Look at these three situations:

- A team of scientists tries to determine the effects of a new medicine.
- A baby accidentally drops her spoon. Dad comes to pick it up. The baby drops the spoon ten more times.
- You and your friends have a taste test for ice cream.

All of these are experiments. They are done carefully and involve trial and error.

Name: ______________________________ Date: ______________

Divide and Conquer:
Prefixes e- and ex-

Directions: Complete the chart below. Put the roots together to make a definition for each word. Be sure to use *out* in your definition.

Word	Prefix Means	Base Means	Definition
1. explode		*plod-* = burst	
2. exclaim		*claim-* = shout, cry	
3. extend		*tend-* = stretch	
4. erode		*rod-* = chew, gnaw	
5. exclude		*clud-* = shut, close	

6. With your partner, write sentences using at least three of these words.

____

____

____

Name: ____________________ Date: ____________

Making Connections:
Guess My Picture!

Directions: Make a drawing that shows the meaning of each sentence below. Share your drawings with a partner. Ask your partner to match the drawings with the sentences.

1. The balloon *exploded* because we put too much air in it.
2. The *exhaust* from automobiles can make walking along city streets unpleasant.
3. The hillside soil was *eroded* by the downpour.
4. Volcanoes in the Hawaiian Islands continue to *erupt*.

1.	2.
3.	4.

Directional Prefix *in-*

in- = "in", "on", "into"

Standards

Uses phonetic and structural analysis techniques, syntactic structure, and semantic context to decode unknown words

Determines the meaning of the new word formed when a known root is added to a known word

Materials

- *About the Root: Directional Prefix* in- (pages 60–61)
- *Divide and Conquer: Directional Prefix* in- (page 62)
- *Making Connections:* Is It "In" or Is It "Not"? (page 63)

Teaching Tips

- The Latin directional prefix *in-* means "in," "on," or "into." For example, to *inhabit* means to live "in" a dwelling or environment; to *inhale* means to breathe "in." The directional prefix *in-* attaches to many whole words (e.g., *indoors, inside, input*) and to many Latin bases that are not whole words (e.g., *inhale, insert, inspect*).
- Although the negative prefix *in-* and the directional prefix *in-* are spelled identically, students can avoid confusing them by asking, "Does this word mean 'not' or 'in'?" The final activity of this lesson gives students practice in distinguishing negative *in-* from directional *in-*.

Guided Practice

About the Root: Directional Prefix *in-*

1. Write these pairs of words on the board: *inhale/exhale* and *inside/outside*. Ask students to talk with partners to figure out the difference between the two words in each pair. (The words are antonyms, or opposites.) Although the words in each pair contain the same base (*-hale* and *-side*), their prefixes differ and make them opposite in meaning. Explain that the prefix *in-* means "in," "on," or "into." Then ask partners to talk about where the "in" is in *inhale* and *inside*. Invite sharing.

2. Remind students that *in-* can also mean "not." Explain that students need to think about words beginning with these prefixes and that they should ask themselves, "Is this word negative, or does it have something to do with 'in'?"

Directional Prefix *in-* (cont.)

3. Ask students to complete the About the Root pages. They can work individually or with partners. After they have finished, invite whole-group conversation. Students can share answers, talk about the text passage, or generate more words containing the root.

4. After students have discussed the Activate questions, invite whole-group conversation. You may wish to have students write down the shared ideas to revisit at a later time.

Divide and Conquer: Directional Prefix *in-*

5. As you guide students through Divide and Conquer, use the questions below to generate discussion about each of the words:

   - Where is the meaning of "in," "on," or "into" in the word ______?
   - Where might you see the word ______?
   - Can you think of an example of ______?
   - Does ______ have more than one meaning? If so, how are those meanings the same? How are they different?
   - How is the word ______ different from the word ______?

   Note: The suffix *-able* means "able to be." Help students see how the suffix contributes to meaning.

Making Connections: Is It "In" or Is It "Not"?

6. Have students complete this activity alone or with partners. To conclude this activity, invite sharing.

Words with *in-* (directional)

incise	ingest
incised	ingested
incising	ingesting
incisor	ingredient
incline	ingrowth
inclination	inhabit
inclined	inhabitant
inclining	inhale
indicate	inhaled
indication	inhaling
indicated	inhalation
indicating	inherit
indicator	inheritance
indigenous	inherited
inductive	inheriting
induce	innate
induced	inoculate
inducing	inoculated
inert	inoculating
infect	inoculation
infected	insect
infecting	insecticide
infection	instinct
infiltration	intake
inflammable	internal

To print a full list of words for students, see page 150.

Name: ______________________ Date: ____________

About the Root:
Directional Prefix *in-*

Activate

Directions: Share a new version of the sentences below with a partner.

Example
The scientist measured the monkey's water intake.
New Version: The scientist measured the water the monkey took in.

1. I had an ingrown toenail. It hurt!
2. Some of people's personalities are innate.
(**Hint**: *nat-* means "born.")

Respond

Directions: Read the passage on page 61. Then answer the question below.

3. The two roots in the word *inject* are *in-* and *-ject*, which means "throw." Explain what these roots tell us about the meaning of *inject*.

____

____

____

____

About the Root:
Directional Prefix *in-* *(cont.)*

Inoculations

Have you ever had a flu shot or a tetanus shot? If so, you have been inoculated. This is a fancy word that describes giving a human or animal something that grows or reproduces inside the body. This is done to protect the human or animal from diseases. Inoculations may be injected. Sometimes, the inoculation, or vaccine, comes in the form of a drink.

The idea of trying to keep people healthy in this way is very old. In fact, India and China used inoculations in the eighth and tenth centuries. In both cases, they were trying to keep people from getting smallpox, a deadly disease.

By the way, did you know that the Latin base *ocul-* means "eye"? When we are *inoculated*, the doctor makes a very tiny hole, or "eye," in our skin by puncturing it with a needle. The vaccine is injected "in the eye," which is the tiny hole!

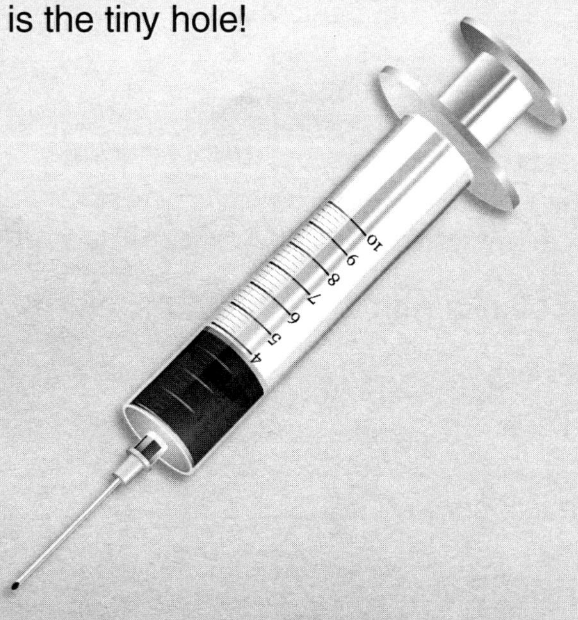

Name: ______________________________ Date: ______________

Divide and Conquer:

Directional Prefix *in-*

Directions: Complete the chart below. Put the roots together to make a definition for each word. Be sure to use *on*, *in*, or *into* in your definition.

Word	Prefix Means	Base Means	Definition
1. inspect		*spect-* = look, watch	
2. inflate		*flat-* = blow	
3. inflammable		*flam-* = flame	
4. inhale		*hal-* = breathe	
5. induct		*duct-* = lead	

Directions: Fill in the blanks with words from the chart.

6. Some people like to ________________ new friends into a group.

7. Scientists use microscopes to ________________ cells.

8. Contractors sometimes wear masks so they won't ________________ dangerous fumes.

Name: ______________________________ Date: ______________

Making Connections:

Is It "In" or Is It "Not"?

Directions: Work with a partner. Use five words from the Word Bank to complete the sentences below. Then place all of the words into the correct column.

Word Bank

inaccurate	inhumane	insert	indirect
insufficient	ingest	innate	invincible
inclined	invasion	incorrect	infected

1. Animals usually ______________ food only when they are hungry, but people sometimes don't.
2. The ______________ of foreign animals and plants, like zebra mussels, is harming some lakes.
3. All living creatures have an ______________ desire for survival.
4. Wheel chair ramps are ______________ planes.
5. ______________ the chemicals into the test tube.

Directional Prefix means "in," "on," "into"	Negative Prefix means "not"
______________	______________
______________	______________
______________	______________
______________	______________
______________	______________
______________	______________

Prefix *sub-*

sub- = "under", "below"

Standards

Uses a variety of context clues to decode unknown words

Uses a known root word as a clue to the meaning of an unknown word with the same root

Materials

- *About the Root: Prefix* sub- (pages 66–67)
- *Divide and Conquer: Prefix* sub- (page 68)
- *Making Connections:* Sub- *Words* (page 69)

Teaching Tips

- *Sub-* means "under" or "below." *Sub-* attaches to whole words (e.g., *subzero*) and Latin bases (e.g., *submerge*).
- This prefix indicates the direction of "under" and "below" in a literal sense: a *submarine* travels under the surface of the water; a *subfloor* lies under the floor covering; *subtitles* run under the images on a movie or television screen; a *substructure* lies beneath the superstructure imposed above it.
- The prefix *sub-* is also used in words indicating a measurement or level that falls "below an established standard." A below-level performance may be deemed *substandard*; *subzero* temperatures fall below a set reference point; in the theory of evolution, gorillas and other primates are considered *subhuman* because they fall below the reference point of complete human development.

Guided Practice

About the Root: Prefix *sub-*

1. Review the concept of prefix (a unit added to the front of a word that changes its meaning; many prefixes are directional in force). Write the word *submarine* on the board. Ask students where a submarine travels. Point out that a submarine travels "under" the surface of the water. Tell students that marine means "sea," so a submarine is literally a boat that travels "under" the "sea." Explain that *sub-* is a prefix meaning "under" or "below." Draw a line between *sub-* and *marine* to draw students' attention to how the word is built.

Prefix sub- *(cont.)*

2. Write *subzero* on the board. Ask students what a *subzero* temperature is. Point out that a subzero temperature is "below" zero. Draw a line between *sub-* and *zero* to draw students' attention to how the word is built.

3. Have students complete the About the Root pages. They can work individually or with partners. After they have finished, invite whole-group conversation. Students can share answers, talk about the text passage, or generate more words containing the root.

4. After students have discussed the Activate questions, invite whole-group conversation. You may wish to have students write down the shared ideas to revisit at a later time.

Divide and Conquer: Prefix sub-

5. As you guide students through Divide and Conquer, use the questions below to generate discussion about each of the words:

    - Where is the meaning of "under" or "below" in the word ______?
    - Where might you see the word ______?
    - Can you think of an example of ______?
    - Does ______ have more than one meaning? If so, how are those meanings the same? How are they different?
    - How is the word ______ different from the word ______?

    Note: The suffixes *-an* and *-al* make their words adjectives. Help students see how the suffixes contribute to meaning.

Making Connections: Sub- Words

6. To conclude this activity, invite students to share their explanations for how the words mean "under" or "below." Clarify, as needed.

Words with sub-

subaerial
subaquatic
subatmospheric
subcelestial
subclass
subcortex
subhuman
subglacial
submarine
submerge
submerged
submerging
suboceanic
subsolar
subsonic
substance
substantive
substruct
subsurface
subsume
subsumed
subsuming
subterranean
subtract
subtracted
subtracting
subzero

To print a full list of words for students, see page 151.

Name: ______________________________ Date: ______________

About the Root:
Prefix *sub-*

Activate

Directions: Think about how *subterranean*, *submerge*, and *subhuman* can be used to complete the sentences below. Then discuss them with a partner.

1. When it gets very hot outside, I like to __________________ myself in a cool bath.
2. Gorillas are __________________ primates.
3. All earthquakes are __________________ because they take place below the Earth's surface.

Respond

Directions: Read the passage on page 67. Then answer the questions below.

4. What would you do if you thought subterranean termites were around your house?

____

____

5. In what part of a large city would you find subways? Why?

____

____

About the Root:
Prefix *sub-* (cont.)

Subterranean Termites

You may have heard of termites. They are tiny but very destructive insects found in all parts of the United States. They are very small ($\frac{1}{8}$ inch to 1 inch in size). Yet they can eat an entire building! Each insect eats tiny pieces of wood using its saw-like jaws. But termites live in colonies of up to two million, so all of those tiny jaws can cause quite a mess!

As you might guess by their name, subterranean termites live underground. They build tiny tunnels called *mud tubes* to get to the wood they eat. They can make their way up from the substructure of a building, eat their way through the subfloor, and continue to climb to the roof. Like subways found in large cities, the mud tubes that termites build extend almost anywhere—even through cracks in concrete.

Name: ______________________________ Date: ______________

Divide and Conquer:
Prefix sub-

Directions: Complete the chart below. Put the roots together to make a definition for each word. Be sure to use *under* or *below* in your definition.

Word	Prefix Means	Base Means	Definition
1. submerge		*merge-* = plunge, dip	
2. subterranean		*terra-* = earth	
3. subnormal		*norm-* = norm	
4. subside		*side-* = sit, settle	
5. subtract		*tract-* = pull, draw, drag	

6. How are *submerge* and *subterranean* the same? How are they different?

____

____

____

Name: ______________________________ Date: ______________

Making Connections:
Sub- Words

Directions: Work with a partner to complete the chart below. Combine the prefix *sub-* with the words or word parts from the Word Bank that best fits the described situation in the left column. Then explain how the word you chose includes the ideas of "under" or "below" in the right column.

Word Bank		
human	standard	way
marine	traction	zero

The Situation	How the Word Means "Under" or "Below"
1. Many big cities have underground train systems so people can get around without cars: ____________	
2. During the blizzard, the temperature outside dropped below zero: ____________	
3. I forgot to do my science homework, so I quickly completed it on the way to school. When I turned it in, my teacher told me it was below the standard quality of my usual work: ____________	
4. "Four take away two is two": ____________	
5. Dogs and cats are mammals, but they are not as smart as humans: ____________	
6. In the Navy, sailors learn how to drive these underwater vessels: ____________	

Prefixes *semi-* and *hemi-*

***semi-*, *hemi-* = "half," "partial"**

Standards

Uses phonetic and structural analysis techniques, syntactic structure, and semantic context to decode unknown words

Determines the meaning of general academic and domain-specific words and phrases in a text relevant to a grade 3 topic or subject area

Materials

- *About the Root: Prefixes* semi- *and* hemi- (pages 72–73)
- *Divide and Conquer: Prefixes* semi- *and* hemi- (page 74)
- *Making Connections: Scrambles* (page 75)

Teaching Tips

- The prefixes *semi-* and *hemi-* mean "half" or "partial." These prefixes may be attached to words with or without hyphens (e.g., *semidarkness, semi-conscious*). Whether a hyphen is used or is not, the meaning of the prefixes remains the same.
- The Latin prefix *semi-* appears in a large number of academic words. The precise meaning of "half" is clear in such words as *semicircle* (a half circle), *semiannual* (occurring every half year), and *semimonthly* (occurring every half month). The meaning of "partial" is clear in such words as *semicolon* (punctuation mark indicating a partial colon), *semiaquatic* (describing plants that live near water but are not fully aquatic), and *semiprecious* (describing gems which are not fully precious). Students can use either of the meanings of "half" and "partial" when they encounter these words.
- The Greek prefix *hemi-* appears in the important science word *hemisphere,* describing half of the globe or sphere of the Earth.

Guided Practice

About the Root: Prefixes *semi-* and *hemi-*

1. Draw a circle and a semicircle on the board. Label each figure. Ask students to talk with partners to determine what *semi-* means. As they share, tell them that *semi-* can mean "half."

2. Tell students to imagine a time during the day when it is almost dark. Tell them that this can be called *semidarkness*. Again, ask partners to figure out what *semi-* means. As they share, tell them that *semi-* can also mean "partial."

Prefixes *semi-* and *hemi-* (cont.)

3. Explain that the prefix *hemi-* can also mean "half" or "partial." Draw their attention to hemispheres on the globe as an example.

4. Ask students to complete the About the Root pages. They can work individually or with partners. After they have finished, invite whole-group conversation. Students can share answers, talk about the text passage, or generate more words containing the root.

5. After students have discussed the Activate questions, invite whole-group conversation. You may wish to have students write down the shared ideas to revisit at a later time.

Divide and Conquer: Prefixes *semi-* and *hemi-*

6. As you guide students through Divide and Conquer, use the questions below to generate discussion about each of the words:

   - Where is the meaning of "half" or "partial" in the word ______?
   - Where might you see the word ______?
   - Can you think of an example of ______?
   - Does ______ have more than one meaning? If so, how are those meanings the same? How are they different?
   - How is the word ______ different from the word ______?

   Note: The suffixes in this exercise make words adjectives. Help students see how the suffixes contribute to meaning.

Making Connections: Scrambles

7. Have students work alone or with partners.

8. To conclude this activity, invite sharing. You may wish to post students' sketches on a bulletin board.

Words with *semi-* and *hemi-*

hemicycle	semidarkness
hemihydrate	semifinal
hemihydrated	semiformed
hemisphere	semilunar
hemispheric	semiliquid
hemispherical	semiprecious
semiabstract	semiskilled
semicircle	semisolid
semicircular	semispherical
semiconductor	semitransparent
semiconsciousness	semitropical

To print a full list of words for students, see page 151.

Name: ______________________________ Date: ______________

About the Root:
Prefixes *semi-* and *hemi-*

Activate

Directions: Think about the questions below. Discuss them with a partner.

1. Of the foods applesauce, apple pie, and caramel apple, which one is *semisolid*? Why?

2. Label the Northern Hemisphere and the Southern Hemisphere on the globe. What does *hemi-* mean?

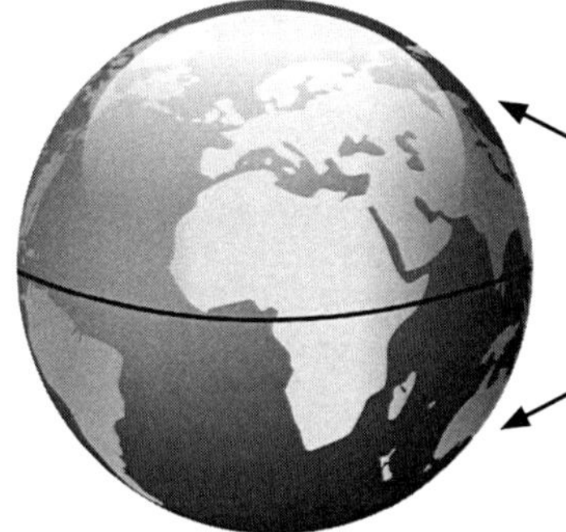

____

____

Respond

Directions: Read the passage on page 73. Then answer the question below.

3. *Semi-* means "half" or "partial." Use an example from the text to explain how *semi-* adds to the meaning of *semiconductor*.

____

____

____

About the Root:
Prefixes *semi-* and *hemi-* *(cont.)*

Semiconductors

You may know that some metals, such as silver or copper, conduct electricity. Materials called *insulators* do not conduct electricity. Rubber is an example of an insulator.

Somewhere between conductors and insulators are devices called *semiconductors*. Scientists can control the amount of electricity that flows through semiconductors. Heat is one way to do this. As the heat increases, the flow of electricity increases. The colder the temperature, the lower the flow of electricity. Impurities added to semiconductor blocks also slow the flow of electricity.

Semiconductors are important in today's life. Anything that is computerized relies on semiconductors. Anything that uses radio waves also relies on them.

Name: ______________________________ Date: ________________

Divide and Conquer:

Prefixes *semi-* and *hemi-*

Directions: Complete the chart below. Put the roots together to make a definition for each word. Be sure to use *half* or *partial* in your definition.

Word	Prefix Means	Base Means	Definition
1. semiannual		*annu-* = year	
2. semiaquatic		*aqua-* = water	
3. hemisphere		*sphere-* = globe	
4. semicircular		circle	
5. semiprecious		*preci-* = value	

6. Talk with a partner. Think about the words above in science. Write a sentence or two about science using some of the words.

____

____

____

Name: ______________________________ Date: ______________

Making Connections:
Scrambles

Directions: Unscramble the words to fill in the blanks.

1. The diameter divides a circle into two ______________. (semicceilrs)
2. Nocturnal animals begin activity in the ______________. (semiadeknrss)
3. Otters and hippopotamuses are ______________ animals. Sometimes they live on land, and sometimes they live in the water. (semiaaciqtu)
4. The Northern and Southern ______________ are divided by the equator. (hemieehprss)
5. Matter that is partially liquid and partially solid is called ______________. (semidiilqu)
6. When the patient got to the hospital, he was ______________. The doctor told his family that he was only partially alert. (semiccinoosus)
7. Select two of the words from the blanks above. Make sketches of them. Trade papers with a partner. See if your partner can guess which words you sketched.

Base *vid-, vis-*

vid-, vis- **= "see"**

Standards

Uses a variety of context clues to decode unknown words

Identifies and knows the meaning of the most common prefixes and derivational suffixes

Materials

- *About the Root: Base* vid-, vis- (pages 78–79)
- *Divide and Conquer: Base* vid-, vis- (page 80)
- *Making Connections: Riddle Time!* (page 81)

Teaching Tips

- The Latin base *vid-, vis-* means "see." You may want to remind students that bases give a word its core or base meaning. This base appears in many important words from everyday language and from science, including some we may not automatically associate with "seeing." For example, when we *visit* friends, we go and see them. When we *revise* our papers, we change them after we have seen them again and taken a second look. When we shop for weekly *provisions* at the grocery store to *provide* food for the table, we are seeing ahead to next week's needs.
- In science, important *vid-* and *vis-* words include *vision, visual, visible*, and *invisible*. Other important words include *supervise* (to oversee a project), *evident* and *evidence* (describing factual matters that make things clear to see).

Guided Practice

About the Root: Base *vid-, vis-*

1. Write the words *visible* and *invisible* on the board. Ask students to work with partners to a) define the words and b) list some things that are visible and invisible. Invite sharing. As students define the words, stress the basic idea of "seeing" in these words. As students suggest things that are visible or invisible, make a T-chart (*visible, invisible*) on the board and stress the notion of seeing. Tell students that *vid-* and *vis-* are two forms of the Latin base that means "see."

2. Ask students to complete the About the Root pages. They can work individually or with partners. After they have finished, invite whole-group conversation. Students can share answers, talk about the text passage,

Base *vid-*, *vis-* (cont.)

or generate more words containing the root.

3. After students have discussed the Activate questions, invite whole-group conversation. You may wish to have students write down the shared ideas to revisit at a later time.

Divide and Conquer: Base *vid-*, *vis-*

4. As you guide students through Divide and Conquer, use the questions below to generate discussion about each of the words:

   - Where is the meaning of "see" in the word ______?
   - Where might you see the word ______?
   - Can you think of an example of ______?
   - Does ______ have more than one meaning? If so, how are those meanings the same? How are they different?
   - How is the word ______ different from the word ______?

   Note: The suffix *-ion* makes a word a noun. Help students see how the suffix contributes to meaning.

Making Connections: Riddle Time!

5. To conclude this activity, invite sharing.

6. Students can sketch the words that they used for their skits and have others guess the word being portrayed.

Words with *vid-* and *vis-*

envision	supervise
envisioned	supervised
envisioning	supervising
evident	supervision
evidence	supervisor
improvise	televise
improvisation	televised
improvised	televising
improvising	television
invisible	unrevised
nonvisual	unsupervised
provide	video
providence	videography
provident	visible
provisions	vision
revise	visit
revised	visited
revising	visiting
revision	visitor
revisit	visual acuity
revisited	visualize
revisiting	

To print a full list of words for students, see page 152.

Name: ______________________________ Date: ______________

About the Root:
Base *vid-*, *vis-*

Activate

Directions: Think about the questions below. Discuss them with a partner.

1. How does the word *video*, as in video camera, include the idea of "seeing"?
2. What might the *visual* display of the results of an experiment look like?

Respond

Directions: Read the passage on page 79. Then answer the questions below.

3. Why do you think the idea of a television caught on so quickly?

____

____

____

4. Do you think we live in a video world? Why or why not?

____

____

____

About the Root:
Base *vid-*, *vis-* *(cont.)*

Television

The word *television* comes from two roots. *Tele-* comes from Greek. It means "far" or "far off." *Vis-* comes from Latin. It means "see." So a television lets us see things from far away.

The first use of the word *television* came at the 1900 World Fair in Paris, France. Scientists showed how electricity might one day be used. One use was to send images out through electric wires.

But it took many more years of work with the idea of television before it was actually invented. It wasn't until 1927 that scientists were able to beam a picture between Washington, D.C. and New York City. After that, television technology grew quickly. In 1936, there were only 200 sets being used worldwide. In 2003, there were nearly one and one-half billion. It is evident that we live in a video world.

Name: ______________________ Date: ____________

Divide and Conquer:
Base *vid-*, *vis-*

Directions: Complete the chart below. An *X* means that the word has no prefix. Put the roots together to make a definition for each word. Be sure to use *see* in your definition.

Word	Prefix Means	Base Means	Definition
1. revision	*re-* = back, again		
2. provisions	*pro-* = forward, ahead		
3. visit	X		
4. visor	X		
5. evident	*e-* = out, very		

Directions: Use some of the words from the chart to fill in the blanks.

6. It is self-________________ that things equal to the same thing are equal to each other.

7. The teacher told me to take a second look at my paper and to submit a ________________.

8. In anticipation of the looming power outage, the local residents were stocking up on their ________________.

Name: ______________________ Date: ______________

Making Connections:
Riddle Time!

Directions: Read the clues. Solve the riddles. Then create a skit to represent one of the words to share with a partner.

1. I have four syllables.

   I am a thing.

   You can see things from far away using me.

   You may watch shows on me.

   What am I?

2. I have three syllables.

   I do not have a prefix, but I have a suffix.

   My suffix means "able to be."

   I describe something that is able to be seen.

   What am I?

3. I have four syllables.

   I have a prefix and a suffix.

   My prefix means "not."

   I am the opposite of #2.

   What am I?

   ____

4. Choose one of the following words: *vision, visitor, video, supervisor.* Write your own riddle on a separate sheet of paper. Ask your partner to solve the riddle.

Name: ______________________________ Date: ______________

Unit II Review:

Science Crossword Puzzle

Directions: Use the words in the Word Bank and the clues to complete the crossword puzzle on page 83.

Word Bank

exclaim	inhale	semicircle	subzero
exhale	inspect	semisolid	television
hemisphere	invisible	subhuman	visualize
inflammable		subterranean	

Across

7. All animals, except people, can be called ______.
9. ______ earthquakes and volcanoes can cause trouble on Earth's surface.
10. We frequently ______ the lab to make sure everything is safe.
11. ______ matter is neither liquid nor solid.
12. When we ______, air enters our lungs.
13. Archimedes ______ed "Eureka!" when he discovered the effect of water on weight.
14. Few plants and animals thrive in ______ temperatures.

Down

1. Some things do not catch on fire, but some things are ______.
2. After the radio, ______ was an important media invention.
3. Computer images can help us ______ abstract scientific things.
4. A ______ is half a circle.
5. When we ______, air leaves our lungs.
6. Microscopes allow us to see things that are ______ to the naked eye.
8. The equator is an imaginary line between the Northern and Southern ______s.

Name: ____________________ Date: __________

Unit II Review:
Science Crossword Puzzle

Directions: Use the words from the Word Bank and the clues on page 82 to complete the crossword puzzle below.

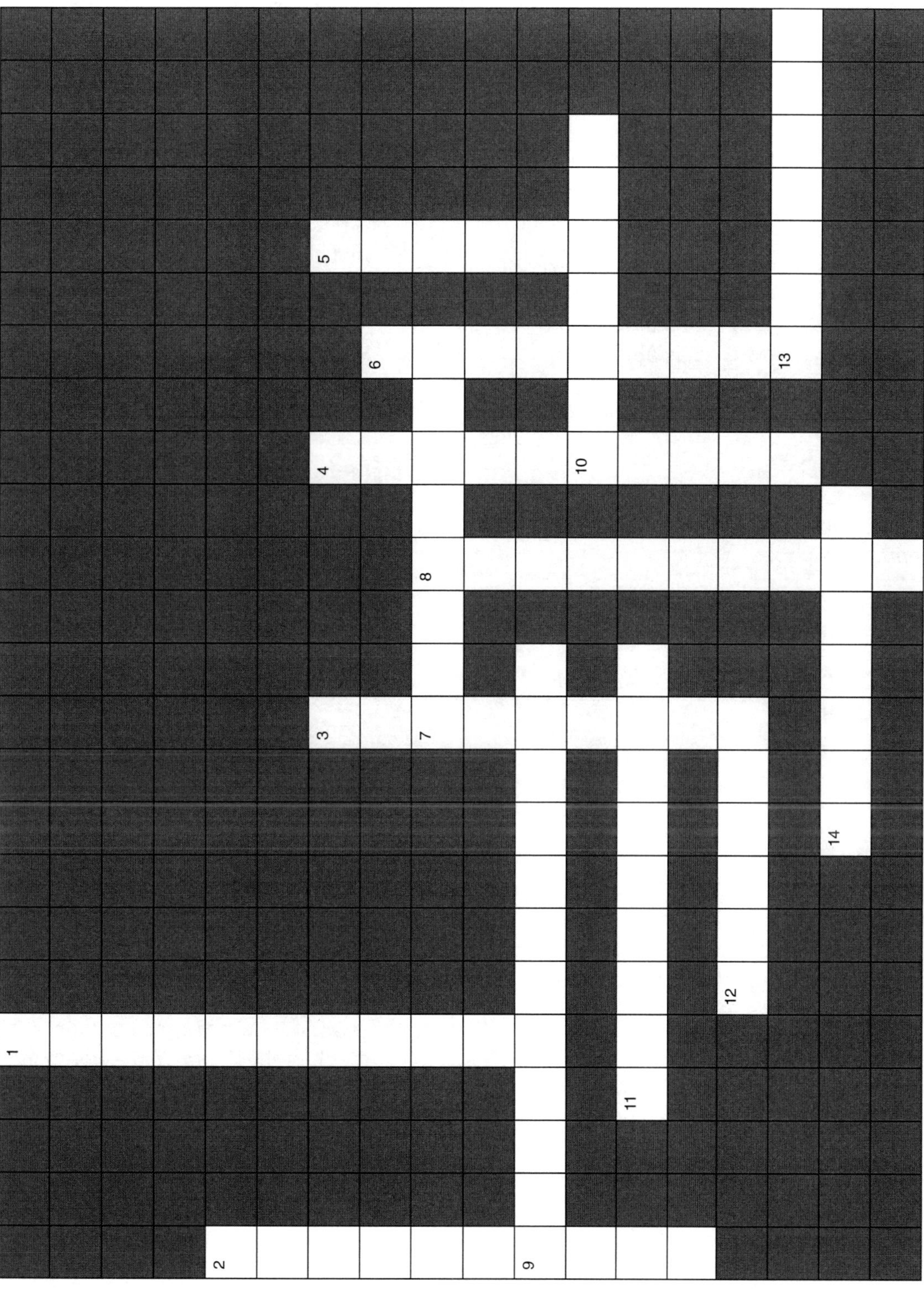

Numerical Prefixes *uni-* and *unit-*

***uni-* and *unit-* = "one", "single"**

Standards

Uses phonetic and structural analysis techniques, syntactic structure, and semantic context to decode unknown words

Determines the meaning of the new word formed when a known root is added to a known word

Materials

- *About the Root: Numerical Prefixes* uni- *and* unit- (pages 86–87)
- *Divide and Conquer: Numerical Prefixes* uni- *and* unit- (page 88)
- *Making Connections:* Uni- *Scramble* (page 89)

Teaching Tips

- The prefixes *uni-* and *unit-* mean "one" or "single." *Uni-* attaches both to intact words (e.g., *unicycle*, *uniform*) and to Latin bases that are not whole words (e.g., *unify, unilateral*).
- In some words, the prefix *uni-* or *unit-* is the only root. In these instances, the prefix functions like a base, providing the word with its essential meaning. For example, in words such as *unit* (a group of one, a single item) or *unite* (to form one thing or group out of many) the roots *uni-* and *unit-* provide the base meaning.
- When you present *uni-* and *unit-* to your students, focus their attention on the concept of "one" or "single" in each of the words. Students do not need to know whether *uni-, unit-* functions as a prefix or as a base in the words they work with. Remember: The goal of the roots approach is to have students look inside the word for meaning.
- If students confuse the negative prefix *un-* with the numerical prefix *uni-*, simply ask them to pronounce the words out loud. The prefix in all negative *un-* words (e.g., *unable*) is pronounced with the short /u/ sound (rhyming with *bun*). The numerical prefixes *uni-* and *unit-,* by contrast, are always pronounced with the long /u/ sound (as in *use*).

Guided Practice

About the Root: Numerical Prefixes *uni-* and *unit-*

1. Show students a picture of a unicorn and write the word on the board. Invite description. Accept responses, but when someone says, "It has a horn," draw a slash after *uni-*. Explain that the *uni-* in *unicorn* refers to its "one" horn.

2. Tell students that in all words beginning with *uni-*, the prefix is pronounced to sound like the *u* in *you* or *use*. Write a few more *uni-* words on the board and ask students to say them out loud, stretching out the long /u/ sounds (e.g., United States of America, a school uniform.) Ask students, "How does each of these *uni-*, *unit-* words mean 'one'?" (The United States is "one" or a "single" nation out of many states; a uniform is a "single" or "one" type of clothing worn by people in a profession.)

Numerical Prefixes *uni-* and *unit-* *(cont.)*

3. If you believe students will confuse *uni-* and *unit-* with the negative prefix *un-*, write the word *unable* on the board. Ask students to pronounce it aloud. Point out that in all words beginning with *un-*, the prefix is pronounced to rhyme with *bun*. Remind students that it is often helpful to pronounce *uni-* and *unit-* words out loud and then ask themselves, "How does this word mean 'one' or 'single'?"

4. Ask students to complete the About the Root pages. They can work individually or with partners. After they have finished, invite whole-group conversation. Students can share answers, talk about the text passage, or generate more words containing the root.

5. After students have discussed the Activate questions, invite whole-group conversation. You may wish to have students write down the shared ideas to revisit at a later time.

Words with *uni-* and *unit-*

E Pluribus Unum	uniformed
unicelled	unify
unicellular	unified
unicolor	unifiying
unicolored	union
unicorn	unison
unicycle	unit
unification	unite
uniform	united
	uniting

To print a full list of words for students, see page 152.

Divide and Conquer: Numerical Prefixes *uni-* and *unit-*

6. As you guide students through Divide and Conquer, use the questions below to generate discussion about each of the words:

   - Where is the meaning of "one" or "single" in the word ______?
   - Where might you see the word ______?
   - Can you think of an example of ______?
   - Does ______ have more than one meaning? If so, how are those meanings the same? How are they different?
   - How is the word ______ different from the word ______?

Making Connections: *Uni-* Scramble

7. Students can work alone or with partners. To conclude this activity, invite sharing.

Name: ______________________________ Date: ______________

About the Root:

Numerical Prefixes *uni-* and *unit-*

Activate

Directions: Circle the unicycle below. Discuss how you identified the unicycle with a partner.

1.   

Respond

Directions: Read the passage on page 87. Then answer the question below.

2. If a unicycle is considered a simpler machine than a bicycle, why is it harder to ride?

____

____

____

____

____

About the Root:

Numerical Prefixes *uni-* and *unit-* (cont.)

What Is a Unicycle?

Although bicycles are popular throughout the world, some people enjoy riding unicycles. Unicycles have only one wheel. They are machines like bikes. But they are simpler machines.

It's hard to learn to ride a unicycle. Just like bikes, you have to balance left and right. In fact, some people learn to ride unicycles in narrow hallways. That way, they can balance left and right. But front and back balance is also difficult. Your center of gravity needs to be where you want to go.

Even though it is hard to learn to ride a unicycle, many people do. Some people do tricks on their unicycles. They may perform in circuses. Some people even play unicycle basketball or unicycle hockey!

Name: ______________________________ Date: ______________

Divide and Conquer:
Numerical Prefixes *uni-* and *unit-*

Directions: Complete the chart below. An *X* means the word has no prefix. Put the roots together to make a definition for each word. Be sure to use *one* or *single* in your definition.

Word	Prefix Means	Base Means	Definition
1. unicycle		*cycle-* = wheel, circle	
2. unison		*son-* = sound, voice	
3. unify		*fy-* = do, make	
4. unit	X		
5. uniform		*form-* = form, shape	

When we write out numbers, we place them in columns of thousands, hundreds, tens, and ones. We call the "ones" column the "unit" column. In each number listed below, which numeral is in the *unit* column?

6. 2,420 ______________________________

7. 8,576 ______________________________

8. 6,123 ______________________________

9. 3,457 ______________________________

Name: ______________________ Date: ______________

Making Connections:
Uni- Scramble

Directions: Unscramble the words to fill in the blanks. Then use the words from the Word Bank to create your own fill-in-the-blank sentences.

1. The choir sang in ______________. (uninso)
2. Everyone who delivers mail must wear a ______________. (unifmor)
3. A ______________ is not a real animal. (unicnor)
4. At the circus, the clown rode a ______________. (uniccely)
5. America is sometimes called the ______________ States. (Unidet)

Word Bank

uniform united unicolor

6. ______________________________
7. ______________________________
8. ______________________________

Numerical Prefix *bi-*

***bi-* = "two"**

Standards

Uses a variety of context clues to decode unknown words

Uses a known root word as a clue to the meaning of an unknown word with the same root

Materials

- *About the Root: Numerical Prefix* bi- (pages 92–93)
- *Divide and Conquer: Numerical Prefix* bi- (page 94)
- *Making Connections: Two or Not Two?* (page 95)

Teaching Tips

- The prefix *bi-* means "two." *Bi-* attaches to both whole words (*bicycle*) and to Latin bases that are not whole words (*bisect).*
- The meanings of the Latin bases used in this lesson are provided for the student. The objective is for students to internalize the meaning of the prefix *bi-* while working with words that deal with familiar concepts.
- As students brainstorm and suggest *bi-* words meaning "two," they may include such words as *biology* and *biography.* These words begin with the Greek base *bi(o)-*, meaning "life." Ask students to look for the meaning of "two" in all *bi-* words they suggest.

Guided Practice

About the Root: Numerical Prefix *bi-*

1. Write the word *bicycle* on the board, slashing it between *bi-* and *cycle*. Ask students how many wheels a bicycle has. Then ask what the prefix *bi-* means (two).
2. Ask students to raise their hands if they know how to speak more than one language. Write the word *bilingual* on the board. Draw a line between *bi-* and *lingual.* Explain to students that if they know how to speak two languages, they are bilingual. Explain that *-lingu-* is a Latin base meaning "language," so *bilingual* literally means "having two languages."
3. Ask students to complete the About the Root pages. They can work individually or with partners. After they have finished, invite whole-group conversation. Students can share answers, talk about the text passage, or generate more words containing the root.

Numerical Prefix *bi-* *(cont.)*

4. After students have discussed the Activate questions, invite whole-group conversation. You may wish to have students write down the shared ideas to revisit at a later time.

Divide and Conquer: Numerical Prefix *bi-*

5. As you guide students through Divide and Conquer, use the questions below to generate discussion about each of the words:

   - Where is the meaning of "two" in the word ______?
   - Where might you see the word ______?
   - Can you think of an example of ______?
   - Does ______ have more than one meaning? If so, how are those meanings the same? How are they different?
   - How is the word ______ different from the word ______?

   Note: The suffix *-al* makes a word an adjective. Help students see how the suffix contributes to meaning.

Making Connections: Two or Not Two?

6. Have students work alone or with partners.

7. To conclude this activity, invite sharing. Ask students to explain their reasons for categorizing words as they did.

Words with *bi-*

biannual	bimonthly
bicameral	binocular
bicentennial	binoculars
biceps	biped
bicultural	bipeds
bicuspid	biplane
bicycle	bisect
bicycling	bisected
bidirectional	bisecting
biennial	bisection
biennium	bivalve
bifocals	biweekly
bifocal	combine
bilingual	combination
bilingualism	

To print a full list of words for students, see page 153.

Name: ____________________ Date: ____________

About the Root:
Numerical Prefix *bi-*

Activate

Directions: Think about the questions below. Discuss them with a partner.

1. Bipeds walk on two feet. Is a human a biped? Why? Is a dog a biped? Why?
2. Is a person who can speak English and German bilingual? Why?
3. Is a person who speaks German, Spanish, and English bilingual? Why?

Respond

Directions: Read the passage on page 93. Then answer the question below.

4. How many focal points do bifocals have? Cite an example from the text that supports your answer.

____

____

____

____

About the Root:
Numerical Prefix *bi-* (cont.)

Ben's Eyes

Ben Franklin lived over 200 years ago in Philadelphia, Pennsylvania. He was a great American statesman. He was also an inventor. And he had a problem.

As Ben got older, his eyes got weaker. He needed two pairs of eyeglasses. He needed one pair to read and see things up close. The other pair was for seeing things far away. But Ben grew tired of switching his glasses. So he developed a new type of lens that had two focal points. He named his invention the *bifocal*. To see things in the distance, he looked through the top half of the lenses. Through the bottom half, he could see things up close.

Look at the picture of Ben. See the dividing line on each lens of his glasses. The line divides the lenses to provide two (*bi-*) focal points. These were the first bifocals.

Name: ______________________________ Date: ______________

Divide and Conquer:
Numerical Prefix *bi-*

Directions: Complete the chart below. Put the roots together to make a definition for each word. Be sure to use *two* in your definition.

Word	Prefix Means	Base Means	Definition
1. bisect		*sect-* = cut	
2. biannual		*annu-* = year	
3. bilateral		*later-* = side	
4. bilingual		*lingu-* = tongue, language	
5. biped		*ped-* = foot, leg	

6. How would you bisect this circle?

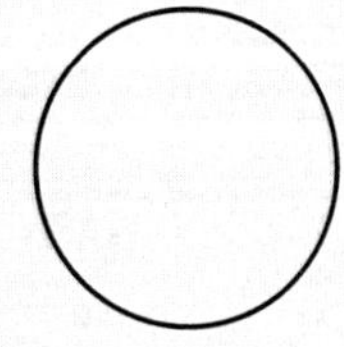

8. How would you bisect this triangle?

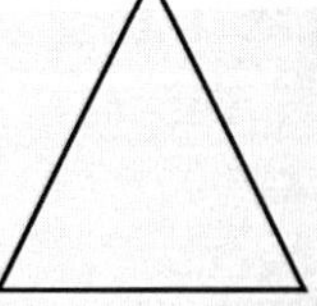

7. How would you bisect this angle?

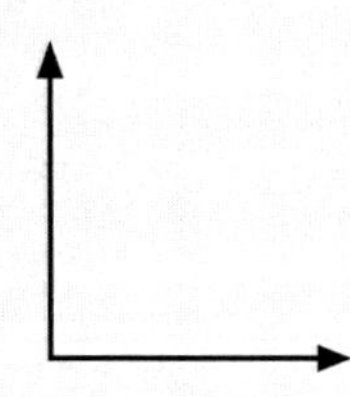

9. How would you bisect this square?

Name: ______________________________ Date: ______________

Making Connections:

Two or Not Two?

Directions: Put each word from the Word Bank into the correct column. Then answer the questions.

Word Bank

bicycle	bisect	birch	bingo
big	biweekly	bimonthly	biped
bill	bifocals	binder	bib

***Bi-* means "two"**	***Bi-* does not mean "two"**
____________________	____________________
____________________	____________________
____________________	____________________
____________________	____________________
____________________	____________________
____________________	____________________

Pick three *bi-* words meaning "two" and fill in the blanks.

1. ______________ means "two" because ______________ .
   ______________________________________ .
2. ______________ means "two" because ______________
   ______________________________________ .
3. ______________ means "two" because ______________
   ______________________________________ .

Numerical Prefix *tri-*

tri- = "three"

Standards

Uses phonetic and structural analysis techniques, syntactic structure, and semantic context to decode unknown words

Determines the meaning of general academic and domain-specific words and phrases in a text relevant to a grade 3 topic or subject area

Materials

- *About the Root: Numerical Prefix* tri- (pages 98–99)
- *Divide and Conquer: Numerical Prefix* tri- (page 100)
- *Making Connections:* Tri- *Riddles* (page 101)

Teaching Tips

The prefix *tri-* means "three." Most students will readily recognize *trio, triplets, tricycle,* and *triangle* as words containing the meaning of "three." *Tri-* attaches to both whole words (*tricycle, triangle*) and to Latin bases that are not whole words (*triplicate, tripod).*

Guided Practice

About the Root: Numerical Prefix *tri-*

1. Ask students, "What is the name for a bike with three wheels?" Write the word *tricycle* on the board, slashing it between *tri-* and *cycle*. Ask students how many wheels are on a tricycle. Then ask what the prefix *tri-* means (three).

2. Draw a large triangle on the board. Ask students how many angles the shape has (three). Then ask them the name of the shape. Write the word *triangle* on the board. Draw a line between *tri-* and *angle* so students can see how the word is divided. Now ask them to explain why this shape is called a triangle (it has three angles).

3. Draw a pair of glasses that contain trifocal lenses. Ask students to explain why this eyeglass is called a trifocal and not a bifocal.

4. Ask students to complete the About the Root pages. They can work individually or with partners. After they have finished, invite whole-group conversation. Students can share answers, talk about the text passage, or generate more words containing the root.

Numerical Prefix *tri-* *(cont.)*

5. After students have discussed the Activate questions, invite whole-group conversation. You may wish to have students write down the shared ideas to revisit at a later time.

Divide and Conquer: Numerical Prefix *tri-*

6. As you guide students through Divide and Conquer, use the questions below to generate discussion about each of the words:

   - Where is the meaning of "three" in the word ______?
   - Where might you see the word ______?
   - Can you think of an example of ______?
   - Does ______ have more than one meaning? If so, how are those meanings the same? How are they different?
   - How is the word ______ different from the word ______?

   Note: The suffixes *-al* and *-ar* make words adjectives. Help students see how the suffixes contribute to meaning.

Making Connections: *Tri-* Riddles

7. Have students work alone or with partners.

8. To conclude this activity, invite sharing. You might ask students to tell where the "three" is in each word.

Words with *tri-*

triangle	trilogies
triangular	trimester
triathlete	trimonthly
triathlon	trio
triceps	triplets
triceratops	triple
tricolor	tripled
tricolored	tripling
tricuspid	triplane
tricycle	triplicate
tricycle	tripod
tricycling	Tripoli
trifocal	trisect
trifocals	trisected
trilingual	trisecting
trilingualism	triweekly
trilogy	

To print a full list of words for students, see page 153.

Name: ______________________________ Date: ______________

About the Root:

Numerical Prefix *tri-*

Activate

Directions: *Tri-* means "three." Discuss with a partner what each word has to do with "three."

tricycle

triplets

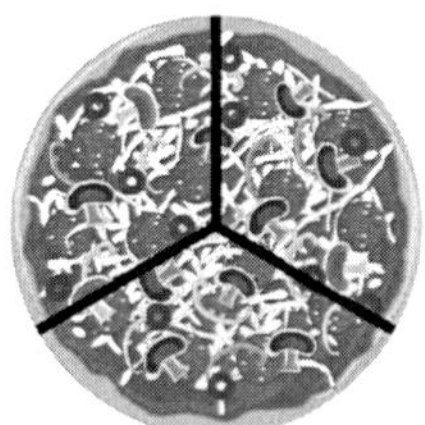

trisected circle

Respond

Directions: Read the passage on page 99. Then answer the questions below.

1. Why do you think it is so hard to win the Triple Crown? ______________________________

____

____

2. A triathlon involves three separate events. How are a Triple Crown and a triathlon alike and different? ______________________________

____

____

____

About the Root:
Numerical Prefix *tri-* *(cont.)*

Triple Crown

Horses like to run. And many people like to watch them run. Horse races are a popular sport around the world. In the 19th century, people in England made a new contest for horses. The horses would run three races. If the same horse won them all, that horse would win the "Triple Crown."

The idea of Triple Crown races caught on. Today, horses race for the Triple Crown in England, Canada, Germany, Chile, Japan, and several other countries.

The United States has Triple Crown races, too. In the spring every year, three-year-old horses can run in the Kentucky Derby, the Belmont Stakes, and the Preakness Stakes. A horse named Sir Barton was the first Triple Crown winner in the United States. He won the races in 1919. We have not had a Triple Crown winner since 1978, when a horse named Affirmed won the races. Like a triathlon, winning the Triple Crown is hard.

Name: ______________________________ Date: ______________

Divide and Conquer:

Numerical Prefix *tri-*

Directions: Complete the chart below. Put the roots together to make a definition for each word. Be sure to use *three* in your definition.

Word	Prefix Means	Base Means	Definition
1. trisect		*sect-* = cut	
2. triannual		*annu-* = year	
3. tripod		*pod-* = foot, leg	
4. triangular		*angle-*, *angul-* = angle	
5. trilingual		*lingu-* = language, tongue	

6. Draw pictures for two of the words above. Show where the "three" is for each picture.

Name: ______________________ Date: __________

Making Connections:
Tri- Riddles

Directions: Use the words from the Word Bank to solve the riddles below. Then create your own riddle.

Word Bank

triceratops tricycle triple trisect

1. I have four syllables.
   I am a dinosaur.
   I have three horns on my head.
   What am I?
   ____

2. I have three syllables.
   I am a riding machine.
   I have three wheels.
   What am I?
   ____

3. I have two syllables.
   My first syllable means "three."
   My second syllable means "cut."
   I mean to cut into three pieces.
   What am I?
   ____

4. I have two syllables.
   I am a hit in baseball.
   Batters who hit me end up on third base.
   What am I?
   ____

5. Choose one of the following words: *tripod*, *triannual*, *triangular*, *trilingual*. Write your own riddle. Ask your partner to solve the riddle.
   ____
   ____
   ____
   ____
   ____
   ____

Numerical Prefixes *quadr-* and *quart-*

***quadr-* and *quart-* = "four," "one-fourth"**

Standards

Uses a variety of context clues to decode unknown words

Identifies and knows the meaning of the most common prefixes and derivational suffixes

Materials

- *About the Root: Numerical Prefixes* quadr- *and* quart- (pages 104–105)
- *Divide and Conquer: Numerical Prefixes* quadr- *and* quart- (page 106)
- *Making Connections: Draw Four* (page 107)

Teaching Tips

- The numerical prefixes *quart-* and *quadr-* mean "four" and also "one-fourth." For example, because a gallon of milk is made up of "four" *quarts*, each of those *quarts* is "one-fourth" of a gallon. When explaining the meaning of this prefix to students, emphasize that the idea of "four" can be four separate things (a *quartet* is made up of "four" people) or one-fourth (a *quarter* is "one-fourth" of a dollar). In words like *quarter* and *quartet*, *quart-* acts like a base.
- This prefix usually attaches to Latin bases that are not whole words (e.g., *quadrilateral, quadruple).* Remember that the objective is for students to internalize the meaning of the prefix *quart-, quadr-* while working with words that deal with familiar concepts.

Guided Practice

About the Root: Numerical Prefixes *quadr-* and *quart-*

1. Write the words *quart*, *quarter,* and *quadrangle* on the board. Show students a gallon container. Ask them how many quarts equal one gallon (4). Write, *A gallon equals four quarts* next to the word *quart*.
2. Show students a one-dollar bill. Ask them how many quarters equal one dollar (4). Write, *A quarter is one-fourth of a dollar* next to the word *quarter.*
3. Draw a quadrangle on the board. Point out that a quadrangle has four angles.
4. Ask students what the words *quarter*, *quart,* and *quadrangle* have in common. Accept responses that note the shared meaning of "four" and the *quart-*, *quadr-* prefix.

Numerical Prefixes *quadr-* and *quart-* (cont.)

5. Return to the words *quarter* and *quadrangle* on the board. Draw a line between *quart-* and *-er* and between *quadr-* and *-angle* to show students how the words are divided. Tell students that both *quart-* and *quadr-* mean "four."

6. Ask students to complete the About the Root pages. They can work individually or with partners. After they have finished, invite whole-group conversation. Students can share answers, talk about the text passage, or generate more words containing the root.

7. After students have discussed the Activate questions, invite whole-group conversation. You may wish to have students write down the shared ideas to revisit at a later time.

Words with *quadr-* and *quart-*

quadrangle	quart
quadrant	quarter
quadrennial	quartered
quadrilateral	quarterback
quadrisect	quarterfinal
quadruple	quartet
quadrupled	quarto
quadrupling	

To print a full list of words for students, see page 154.

Divide and Conquer: Numerical Prefixes *quadr-* and *quart-*

8. As you guide students through Divide and Conquer, use the questions below to generate discussion about each of the words:

   - Where is the meaning of "four" or "one-fourth" in the word ______?
   - Where might you see the word ______?
   - Can you think of an example of ______?
   - Does ______ have more than one meaning? If so, how are those meanings the same? How are they different?
   - How is the word ______ different from the word ______?

   Note: The suffixes *-ar* and *-al* make words adjectives. Help students see how the suffixes contribute to meaning.

Making Connections: Draw Four

9. To conclude this activity, ask students who have sketched the same word to post their sketches. Invite students to compare them. Ask where the "four" is in each sketch.

Name: ______________________________ Date: ______________

About the Root:

Numerical Prefixes *quadr-* and *quart-*

Activate

Directions: Think about the questions below. Discuss them with a partner.

Words that have *quadr-* or *quart-* in them usually have something to do with four.

1. *Quarter* this pizza.

2. Which singing group is a *quartet*? Circle it.

Respond

Directions: Read the passage on page 105. Then answer the question below.

3. Draw a four-sided figure that is not a quadrilateral. Explain how it is not a quadrilateral.

____

____

____

____

About the Root:

Numerical Prefixes *quadr-* and *quart-* (cont.)

What Is a Quadrilateral?

The word part *lateral* means "side." If you know this, you can figure out what a *quadrilateral* is. It is a figure with four sides. Any four-sided shape is a quadrilateral. But the sides have to be straight.

If the four sides are equal, and if all the angles are equal (each 90 degrees), the figure is a square. Draw a square here:	
A rectangle is also a quadrilateral with equal angles (each 90 degrees). Rectangles have two sets of sides. The sides across from each other are equal in length. The two sides in each set are equal, but the sets may not be equal to each other. Draw a rectangle here:	
Even a trapezoid is a quadrilateral. Two sides are parallel. Two sides are not. Draw a trapezoid here:	

Name: ______________________________ Date: ______________

Divide and Conquer:

Numerical Prefixes *quadr-* and *quart-*

Directions: Complete the chart below. *X* means the word has no prefix. Put the roots together to make a definition for each word. Be sure to use *four* or *one-fourth* in your definition.

Word	Prefix Means	Base Means	Definition
1. quadrangular		*angle-*, angul- = angle	
2. quadrisect		*sect-* = cut	
3. quarter	X		
4. quadrennial		*enni-* = year(s)	
5. quart	X		

Directions: Write answers to these questions on a separate sheet of paper.

6. The Summer Olympics are a *quadrennial* event. How often do they happen?
7. How many basketball games are in the *quarterfinals*?
8. How many *quarters* are in a football game?
9. If you want to share your candy bar with three friends and have a piece for yourself, you must give each person a ____________ of it.

Name: ________________________________ Date: ______________

Making Connections:

Draw Four

Directions: Choose three words from the Word Bank. Draw a sketch of each one. Then trade papers. See if a partner can tell which words you chose.

Word Bank

quadrilateral	quart	quadrangle
quadrisect	quarter	quartet

Numerical Prefix *cent-*

cent- = "one hundred," "one one-hundredth"

Standards

Uses phonetic and structural analysis techniques, syntactic structure, and semantic context to decode unknown words

Determines the meaning of the new word formed when a known root is added to a known word

Materials

- *About the Root: Numerical Prefix* cent- (pages 110–111)
- *Divide and Conquer: Numerical Prefix* cent- (page 112)
- *Making Connections: Five Scramble* (page 113)

Teaching Tips

Like *quadr-* and *quart-*, the Latin root *cent-* means "one hundred" or "one one-hundredth." A *century* has 100 years, for example, and a *cent* is $\frac{1}{100}$ of a dollar. *Cent-* appears in many metric measurements. In words from the metric system such as *centimeter, centigram, centiliter*, the Latin prefix *cent-* always means $\frac{1}{100}$ and describes a tiny fraction of a gram, a liter, or a meter.

Guided Practice

About the Root: Numerical Prefix *cent-*

1. Show students a penny, a nickel, a dime, and a dollar bill. Ask what each is called. Write the names on the board. Then write the following: 5 ______ = 1 nickel; 10 ______ = 1 dime; 100 ______ = 1 dollar. Invite students to fill in the blanks. When someone says *cent*, point out that the root *cent-* means 100 (100 cents in a dollar), or $\frac{1}{100}$ (a penny or cent is $\frac{1}{100}$ of a dollar).

2. Ask students what century they are living in. Write the word on the board, and draw a slash after *cent-*. Ask students how many years are in a century.

3. Have students complete the About the Root pages. They can work individually or with partners. After they have finished, invite whole-group conversation. Students can share answers, talk about the text passage, or generate more words containing the root.

4. After students have discussed the Activate questions, invite whole-group conversation. You may wish to have students write down the shared ideas to revisit at a later time.

Numerical Prefix *cent-* (cont.)

Divide and Conquer: Numerical Prefix *cent-*

5. As you guide students through Divide and Conquer, use the questions below to generate discussion about each of the words:

   - Where is the meaning of "100" or "$\frac{1}{100}$" in the word ______?
   - Where might you see the word ______?
   - Can you think of an example of ______?
   - Does ______ have more than one meaning? If so, how are those meanings the same? How are they different?
   - How is the word ______ different from the word ______?

6. Once students have finished the activity, you may wish to have them work with partners to answer the following questions:

   - If a liter is a liquid measurement, then how much liquid is a centiliter? (**Hint:** It is not 100 liters.) ($\frac{1}{100}$ liter)
   - If *bi-* means "two" and *cent-* means "100," how many years are celebrated in a town's *bicentennial*? (200)
   - The celsius scale is a way to measure heat. If 0 *centigrade* is when water freezes, when does water boil? (**Hint:** Think about what *cent-* means.) (100 degrees celcius or centigrade)
   - A gram is a unit of weight. If a paper clip weighs about a gram, what part of the paper clip would weigh a *centigram*? ($\frac{1}{100}$ of a paper clip)

Words with *cent-*

bicentennial	centimeter
cent	centurion
cents	century
centenarian	centuries
centennial	percent
centigrade	percentage
centigram	percentile
centiliter	tricentennial

To print a full list of words for students, see page 154.

Making Connections: Five Scramble

7. Have students work with partners.

8. To conclude this activity, invite sharing. You could also ask students to develop their own scramble sentences using other *cent-* words. They can trade these with partners, who can unscramble the words.

Name: ______________________ Date: ____________

About the Root:

Numerical Prefix *cent-*

Activate

Directions: Think about the questions below. Discuss them with a partner.

Cent- sometimes has something to do with 100.

1. How many *cents* (pennies) in a dollar? ____________

2. Our town had a *bicentennial* celebration. How old is our town? (**Hint**: Remember what *bi-* means) ____________

Respond

Directions: Read the passage on page 111. Then answer the questions below.

3. What century were you born in?____________

4. What century were your parents born in? ____________

5. How do you know the 21st century began in the year 2000?

____

____

About the Root:

Numerical Prefix *cent-* (cont.)

What Is a Century?

A century is 100 years in a row. We are now living in the 21st century. When did the 21st century begin? Some people think that it began January 1, 1999. Almost everyone thinks it is January 1, 2000. So who is right? The first century ran from 0–99. So the year 100 was the start of the second century. With this information, it is clear that the 21st century began in the year 2000.

It is easy to figure out the century for something that happened. You can just add the number one to the first two numbers of the year. For example:

1776, the time of the Revolutionary War, was in the 18th century. (17 + 1 = 18)

World War II took place in the 1930s and 1940s. This is the 20th century. (19 + 1 = 20)

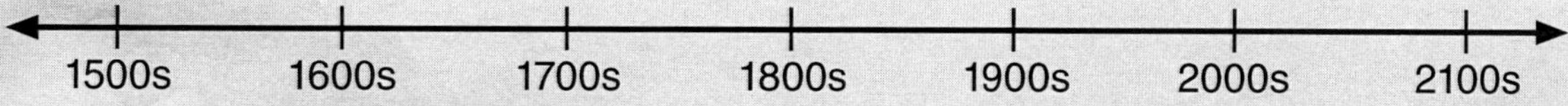

Name: ______________________________ Date: ______________

Divide and Conquer:

Numerical Prefix *cent-*

Directions: Complete the chart below. *X* means the word has no prefix. Put the roots together to make a definition for each word. Be sure to use *one hundred* or *one one-hundredth* in your definition.

Word	Prefix Means	Base Means	Definition
1. centennial		*enni-* = year(s)	
2. centigrade		*grad-* = step, degree	
3. centipede		*ped-* = foot, leg	
4. centimeter		*meter-* = measure, meter	
5. cent	X		

6. In math, a *percentage* is a way of stating numbers. 100 *percent* of something is all of it. 50 *percent* of something is half of it. Would you rather have 50 *percent* of your allowance or 500 *percent* of your allowance? Why? Write your answer on a separate sheet of paper.

Name: ________________________________ Date: ______________

Making Connections:
Five Scramble

Directions: Unscramble the letters to make words that go in the blanks. Use the Word Bank to help you.

Word Bank

bicentennial	centigrade	century	centipede
cent	cents	percent	

1. My grandparents have a home that is as old as a _______________. (rnectuy)
2. Another name for a penny is one _______________. (tecn)
3. If it's 0 degrees _______________ outside, that means it is freezing. (centadegir)
4. I am so happy! I earned a score of 100 _______________ on my test. (petnecr)
5. Our town will soon be 200 years old. The _______________ birthday party will be fun! (bicentaeilnn)
6. An insect with 100 legs is called a _______________. (centeepdi)
7. There are 100 _______________ in a dollar. (censt)

Name: ______________________________ Date: ______________

Unit III Review:

Magic Square Math

Directions: Match the words with their definitions. Then put the numbers of the answers where they belong on the chart. You will know if you are right because each row and each column will add up to the same magic number.

____ **A.** unit	**1.** An amount of weight that is $\frac{1}{100}$ of a gram
____ **B.** bisect	**2.** A geometric figure with three sides and three angles
____ **C.** bimonthly	**3.** To cut into two equal pieces
____ **D.** triangle	**4.** A three-wheeled cycle
____ **E.** tricycle	**5.** Happening every two months
____ **F.** quart	**6.** A geometric figure with four sides and four angles
____ **G.** quadrangle	**7.** A single thing or item
____ **H.** century	**8.** A span of 100 years
____ **I.** centigram	**9.** Four of these make a gallon

A:	**B:**	**C:**
D:	**E:**	**F:**
G:	**H:**	**I:**

Magic Number:

____

Answer Key

Unit I: Lesson 1—Negative Prefix *in-*

About the Root: Negative Prefix *in-* (page 22)

1–4. Students' answers will vary.

Divide and Conquer: Negative Prefix *in-* (page 24)

Students' answers for the "definition" section may vary; accept a range of answers.

1. incorrect = not; correct; not correct, not accurate
2. ineligible = not; eligible; not eligible, not qualified to run for office, not allowed to participate
3. incomplete = not; complete; not complete, not finished, not in the final state
4. inequality = not; equal; (state of) not being equal, (state of) not being fair
5. incredible = not; credible; not credible, not easy to believe, not easy to imagine
6. Students' answers will vary.

Making Connections: *Not* Word Sort (page 25)

Order of answers will vary.

In- means "not"	*In-* does not mean "not"
inactive	inform
inconvenient	inhale
independent	inhabit
ineligible	insist
inexpensive	inspect
involuntary	invitation

Unit I: Lesson 2—Prefix *co-, con-*

About the Root: Prefix *co-, con-* (page 28)

1. Students' answers will vary.
2. copilots; coauthors
3. Students' answers will vary.

Divide and Conquer: Prefix *co-, con-* (page 30)

Students' answers for the "definition" section may vary; accept a range of answers.

1. coauthor = with or together; author; to author together, to write a book with a partner
2. cooperate = with or together; operate; to work together, to get along with others
3. contract = with or together;
4. congregation = with or together; a flocking or gathering together of people to worship, conduct a ceremony, or celebrate with one another
5. construct = with or together; to build together, to take materials and put them together to erect a structure
6. Students' answers will vary.
7. Students' answers will vary.
8. Students' answers will vary.

Making Connections: Draw It! (page 31)

Students' answers will vary.

Unit I: Lesson 3—Prefixes *com-* and *col-*

About the Root: Prefixes *com-* and *col-* (page 34)

1. collector
2. collection
3. composer
4. composition
5. Students' answers will vary.

Answer Key *(cont.)*

Divide and Conquer: Prefixes *com-* and *col-* (page 36)

Students' answers for the "definition" section may vary; accept a range of answers.

1. collide = with or together; to strike or crash together, to make impact with another object
2. compose = with or together; to put things together and arrange them neatly, to put notes together in a musical composition, to put words together in a composed essay
3. collection = with or together; a gathering together of things or people that have been chosen or selected
4. compete = with or together; to seek or pursue a prize along with someone else; to vie with someone else for a prize or award
5. compress = with or together; to squeeze together; as a noun, a *compress* is a folded cloth which has been squeezed together tightly and applied to a source of pain
6. Students' answers will vary.

Making Connections: *Con-* or *Com-*? (page 37)

Order of answers will vary.

con-	*com-*
concentrate	combine
concoct	commune
conduct	compact
confer	companion
conference	compile
construct	compress

com- precedes bases that begin with *b, m,* or *p*

Unit I: Lesson 4—Base *port-*

About the Root: Base *port-* (page 40)

1. to carry across
2. to carry out
3. Students' answers will vary.

Divide and Conquer: Base *port-* (page 42)

Students' answers for the "definition" section may vary; accept a range of answers.

1. export = carry; to carry products and merchandise out of the country, region, or state
2. transport = carry; to carry products from one place to another; to carry items across an area or region
3. porter = carry; a person who carries things such as luggage at a hotel or a train station
4. portage = carry; to carry a canoe across land from one river to another
5. deport = carry; to send out of the country, to remove or "carry off" a person from a country by legal means (**Note:** the prefix *de-* means "removal")
6. Students' answers will vary.

Making Connections: Riddle Me This (page 43)

1. porter
2. portfolio
3. import; export
4. Students' answers will vary.

Unit I: Lesson 5—Bases *mov-*, *mot-*, and *mobil-*

About the Root: Bases *mov-*, *mot-*, and *mobil-* (page 46)

1. mobile
2. motion
3. motor
4. Students' answers will vary.

Answer Key *(cont.)*

Divide and Conquer: Bases *mov-*, *mot-*, and *mobil-* (page 48)

Students' answers for the "definition" section may vary; accept a range of answers.

1. promote = move; to move forward or ahead to the next grade, to move a product forward in sales
2. commotion = move; (state of) many things moving together at the same time
3. mobile = move; able to move, able to be moved
4. motion = move; movement, a proposal for action made in a meeting, motion pictures present moving images
5. remove = move; to move something back or take off, to move something back from where it had been placed
6. Students' answers will vary.
7. Students' answers will vary.

Making Connections: Moving or Not Moving? (page 49)

Has to do with moving	Does not have to do with moving
motel	mote
motion	mother
motivate	motto
motorist	
motorized	

Students' answers will vary.

Unit I Review

Social Studies Crossword Puzzle (pages 50-51)

Across	Down
1. import	1. indivisible
2. collide	4. incomplete
3. involuntary	5. deport
6. collect	6. Congress
9. cooperate	7. transport
10. coworker	8. incorrect
12. coauthors	11. export
13. compete	12. compose

Unit II: Lesson 1—Prefixes *e-* and *ex-*

About the Root: Prefixes *e-* and *ex-* (page 54)

1–3. Students' answers will vary.

Divide and Conquer: Prefixes *e-* and *ex-* (page 56)

Students' answers for the "definition" section may vary; accept a range of answers.

1. explode = out; to burst out in an eruption
2. exclaim = out; to shout out suddenly or in a loud voice, to make an outcry
3. extend = out; to stretch out and lengthen, to make longer in time
4. erode = out; to gnaw or chew away soil by running water, strong winds, or other forces
5. exclude = out; to shut out or close out, to keep someone out of an area or a group
6. Students' answers will vary.

Making Connections: Guess My Picture! (page 57)

Students' answers will vary.

Unit II: Lesson 2—Directional Prefix *in-*

About the Root: Directional Prefix *in-* (page 60)

1–3. Students' answers will vary.

Divide and Conquer: Directional Prefix *in-* (page 62)

Students' answers for the "definition" section may vary; accept a range of answers.

1. inspect = in, on, or into; to look into something and examine it closely
2. inflate = in, on, or into; to blow air into something and enlarge it
3. inflammable = in, on, or into; (able to) burst into flames (**Note:** *inflammable* means "bursting *into* flames" and begins with directional *in-*; by contrast, substances that do not catch fire are called "nonflammable.")
4. inhale = in, on, or into; to breathe in, to take a breath
5. induct = in, on, or into; to lead into a group (e.g., inducted into the Hall of Fame, Armed Forces)
6. induct
7. inspect
8. inhale

Answer Key *(cont.)*

Making Connections: Is It "In" or Is It "Not"? (page 63)

1. ingest
2. invasion
3. innate
4. inclined
5. insert

Directional Prefix means "in," "on," "into"	Negative Prefix means "not"
inclined	inaccurate
ingest	indirect
innate	inhumane
insert	insufficient
invasion	invincible
infected	incorrect

Unit II: Lesson 3—Prefix *sub-*

About the Root: Prefix *sub-* (page 66)

1. submerge
2. subhuman
3. subterranean
4. Students' answers will vary.
5. Students' answers will vary.

Divide and Conquer: Prefix *sub-* (page 68)

Students' answers for the "definition" section may vary; accept a range of answers.

1. submerge = under or below; to plunge under or below water, to dip below the surface of the water
2. subterranean = under or below; under or below the earth's surface
3. subnormal = under or below; below the norm, inferior, not up to the norm
4. subside = under or below; to settle down at a lower level of intensity; (of waters that have risen after a flood or torrent) to return to a lower water level
5. subtract = under or below; to take the lower number away from or "out from under" the higher number
6. Students' answers will vary.

Making Connections: *Sub-* Words (page 69)

1. subway; Students' answers will vary.
2. subzero; Students' answers will vary.
3. substandard; Students' answers will vary.
4. subtraction; Students' answers will vary.
5. subhuman; Students' answers will vary.
6. submarine; Students' answers will vary.

Unit II: Lesson 4—Prefixes *semi-* and *hemi-*

About the Root: Prefixes *semi-* and *hemi-* (page 72)

1–3. Students' answers will vary.

Divide and Conquer: Prefixes *semi-* and *hemi-* (page 74)

Students' answers for the "definition" section may vary; accept a range of answers.

1. semiannual = half or partial; taking place every six months or half-year
2. semiaquatic = half or partial; living near water but not totally in water all the time, living partially in water
3. hemisphere = half or partial; half the sphere of Earth
4. semicircular = half or partial; half circular, shaped like one half of a circle
5. semiprecious = half or partial; not fully precious
6. Students' answers will vary.

Making Connections: Scrambles (page 75)

1. semicircles
2. semidarkness
3. semiaquatic
4. hemispheres
5. semiliquid
6. semiconscious
7. Students' answers will vary.

Answer Key *(cont.)*

Unit II: Lesson 5–Base *vid-*, *vis-*

About the Root: Base *vid-*, *vis-* (page 78)

1–4. Students' answers will vary.

Divide and Conquer: Base *vid-*, *vis-* (page 80)

Students' answers for the "definition" section may vary; accept a range of answers.

1. revision = see; a change made after seeing something again, after taking a second look, we often say, "Take another look at this and see if you can improve it."
2. provisions = see; supplies we take in as we see ahead to future needs, measures we take as we see ahead to a situation in which we will need something, we make provisions for our needs
3. visit = see; to go and see a person or a place
4. visor = see; the bill on a cap which protects our eyes from the sun, in a suit of armor, the face cover on a helmet that protects the eyes but enables the solider to see through, by protecting the eyes, a visor helps us see
5. evident = see; very clear to see, obvious, standing out for all to see
6. evident
7. revision
8. provisions

Making Connections: Riddle Time! (page 81)

1. television
2. visible
3. invisible
4. Students' answers will vary

Unit II Review

Science Crossword Puzzle (pages 82–83)

Across	Down
7. subhuman	**1.** inflammable
9. subterranean	**2.** television
10. inspect	**3.** visualize
11. semisolid	**4.** semicircle
12. inhale	**5.** exhale
13. exclaim	**6.** invisible
14. subzero	**8.** hemisphere

Unit III: Lesson 1–Numerical Prefixes *uni-* and *unit-*

About the Root: Numerical Prefixes *uni-* and *unit-* (page 86)

1. The unicycle represents one wheel.
2. Students' answers will vary.

Divide and Conquer: Numerical Prefixes *uni-* and *unit-* (page 88)

Students' answers for the "definition" section may vary; accept a range of answers.

1. unicycle = one or single; a one-wheeled riding vehicle
2. unison = one or single; spoken or sung in a single voice or with the same musical notes, an agreement shared by many people who are "of one voice"
3. unify = one or single; to organize into a single whole, "to make one"
4. unit = one or single; a single item
5. uniform = one or single; a suit of clothing with one single shape worn by many people
6. 2,420: 0 is in the unit column
7. 8,576: 6 is in the unit column
8. 6,123: 3 is in the unit column
9. 3,457: 7 is in the unit column.

Answer Key *(cont.)*

Making Connections: *Uni-* Scramble (page 89)

1. unison
2. uniform
3. unicorn
4. unicycle
5. United
6. Students' answers will vary.
7. Students' answers will vary.
8. Students' answers will vary.

Unit III: Lesson 2—Numerical Prefix *bi-*

About the Root: Numerical Prefix *bi-* (page 92)

1. yes, humans walk on two legs; no, dogs walk on four legs.
2. yes; they speak two languages.
3. no, they speak more than two languages.
4. two; Students' answers will vary.

Divide and Conquer: Numerical Prefix *bi-* (page 94)

Students' answers for the "definition" section may vary; accept a range of answers

1. bisect = two; to cut or divide into two equal parts, to cut in half
2. biannual = two; taking place two times a year (as opposite to *biennial*, which means "lasting or occurring every two years")
3. bilateral = two; involving two sides or two parties
4. bilingual = two; speaking two languages, writing or written in two languages
5. biped = two; walking on two legs or feet, two-legged
6. Students' answers will vary.
7. Students' answers will vary.
8. Students' answers will vary.
9. Students' answers will vary.

Making Connections: Two or Not Two? (page 95)

Bi- means "two"	*Bi-* does not mean "two"
bicycle	big
bifocals	bill
bimonthly	binder
biped	bingo
bisect	birch
biweekly	bib

1. Students' answers will vary.
2. Students' answers will vary.
3. Students' answers will vary.

Unit III: Lesson 3—Numerical Prefix *tri-*

About the Root: Numerical Prefix *tri-* (page 98)

1. Students' answers will vary.
2. Students' answers will vary.

Divide and Conquer: Numerical Prefix *tri-* (page 100)

Students' answers for the "definition" section may vary; accept a range of answers.

1. trisect = three; to cut or divide into three equal parts, to cut into thirds
2. triannual = three; taking place three times a year (as opposed to *triennial*, which means "lasting or occurring every three years")
3. tripod = three; a three-legged stand
4. triangular = three; containing three angles and three sides
5. trilingual = three; speaking three languages, written in three languages
6. Students' drawings will vary.

Answer Key *(cont.)*

Making Connections: *Tri-* Riddles (page 101)

1. triceratops
2. tricycle
3. trisect
4. triple
5. Students' answers will vary.

Unit III: Lesson 4—Numerical Prefixes *quadr-* and *quart-*

About the Root: Numerical Prefixes *quadr-* and *quart-* (page 104)

1. 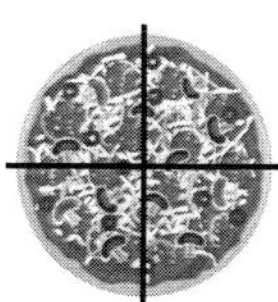

2. 

3. Students' answers will vary.

Divide and Conquer: Numerical Prefixes *quadr-* and *quart-* (page 106)

Students' answers for the "definition" section may vary; accept a range of answers.

1. quadrangular = four; having four angles and therefore also four sides
2. quadrisect = four; to cut or slice into four equal pieces or sections
3. quarter = one-fourth; one-fourth of any amount; a coin that is $\frac{1}{4}$ of a dollar.
4. quadrennial = four; lasting four years; taking place every four years (as opposed to *quarter-annual,* meaning "occurring four times a year")
5. quart = one-fourth; $\frac{1}{4}$ of a gallon
6. every four years
7. four games
8. four quarters
9. fourth; quarter

Making Connections: Draw Four (page 107)

Students' drawings will vary.

Unit III: Lesson 5—Numerical Prefix *cent-*

About the Root: Numerical Prefix *cent-* (page 110)

1. 100 pennies
2. 200 years
3. twenty-first century
4. twentieth century
5. Students' answers will vary.

Divide and Conquer: Numerical Prefix *cent-* (page 112)

Students' answers for the "definition" section may vary; accept a range of answers.

1. centennial = 100; an anniversary marking 100 years
2. centigrade = 100; having 100 degrees between freezing (zero degrees) and boiling (100 degrees)
3. centipede = 100; a 100-legged insect
4. centimeter = $\frac{1}{100}$; $\frac{1}{100}$ meter (about 0.3937 inches)
5. cent = $\frac{1}{100}$; $\frac{1}{100}$ of a dollar
6. 500% because 5 times an amount is larger than $\frac{1}{2}$

Making Connections: Five Scramble (page 113)

1. century
2. cent
3. centigrade
4. percent
5. bicentennial
6. centipede
7. cents

Unit III Review

Magic Square Math (page 114)

A 7	**B** 3	**C** 5
D 2	**E** 4	**F** 9
G 6	**H** 8	**I** 1

Magic Number: 15

References Cited

Baumann, James, Elizabeth C. Carr-Edwards, George Font, Cathleen A. Tereshinski, Edward J. Kame'enui, and Stephen Olejnik. "Teaching Morphemic and Contextual Analysis to Fifth-Grade Students." *Reading Research Quarterly* 37 (2002): 150–176.

Baumann, James F., George Font, Elizabeth C. Edwards, and Eileen Boland. "Strategies for Teaching Middle-Grade Students to Use Word-Part and Context Clues to Expand Reading Vocabulary." In *Teaching and Learning Vocabulary: Bringing Research to Practice*, edited by Elfrieda H. Hiebert and Michael L. Kamil, 179–205. Mahwah, NJ: Erlbaum, 2005.

Bear, Donald, Marcia Invernizzi, Shane Templeton, and Francine R. Johnston. *Words Their Way (5th Edition)*. Upper Saddle River, NJ: Prentice Hall, 2011.

Beck, Isabel L., Margaret G. McKeown, and Linda Kucan. *Bringing Words to Life: Robust Vocabulary Instruction*. New York: Guilford, 2002.

Beck, Isabel, Charles A. Perfetti, and Margaret G. McKeown. "Effects of Long-Term Vocabulary Instruction on Lexical Access and Reading Comprehension." *Journal of Educational Psychology* 74 (1982): 506–521.

Biemiller, Andrew. "Implications for Choosing Words for Primary Grade Vocabulary." In *Teaching and Learning Vocabulary: Bringing Research to Practice*, edited by by Elfrieda H. Hiebert and Michael L. Kamil, 223–242. Mahwah, NJ: Erlbaum, 2005.

Biemiller, Andrew, and Naomi Slonim. "Estimating Root Word Vocabulary Growth in Normative and Advantaged Populations: Evidence for a Common Sequence of Vocabulary Acquisition." *Journal of Educational Psychology* 93 (2001): 498–520.

Blachowicz, Camille, and Peter Fisher. *Teaching Vocabulary in All Classrooms (3rd Edition)*. Upper Saddle River, NJ: Pearson/Merrill/Prentice Hall, 2006.

Blachowicz, Camille, Peter Fisher, Donna Ogle, and Susan Watts-Taffe. "Vocabulary: Questions from the Classroom." *Reading Research Quarterly* 41 (2006): 524–538.

Carlisle, Joanne F. "Awareness of the Structure and Meaning of Morphologically Complex Words: Impact on Reading." *Reading and Writing: An Interdisciplinary Journal* 12 (2000): 169–190.

———. "Effects of Instruction in Morphological Awareness on Literacy Achievement: An Integrative Review." *Reading Research Quarterly* 45 (2010): 464–487.

Chandler, Richard E., and Kessel Schwartz. *A New History of Spanish Literature*. Baton Rouge, LA: LSU Press, 1961/1991.

Cunningham, Patricia M. *Phonics They Use: Words for Reading and Writing*. New York: Longman, 2004.

References Cited *(cont.)*

Graves, M.F., and S.M. Watts-Taffe. "The Place of Word Consciousness in a Research-Based Vocabulary Program." In *What Research Has to Say About Reading Instruction*, edited by Alan E. Farstrup and S. Jay Samuels, 140–165. Newark, DE: International Reading Association, 2002.

Harmon, Janis M., Wanda B. Hedrick, and Karen D. Wood. "Research on Vocabulary Instruction in the Content Areas: Implications for Struggling Readers." *Reading & Writing Quarterly* 21 (2005): 261–280.

Kame'enui, Edward J., Douglas W. Carnine, and Roger Freschi. "Effects of Text Construction and Instructional Procedures for Teaching Word Meanings on Comprehension and Recall." *Reading Research Quarterly* 17 (1982): 367–388.

Kieffer, Michael, and Nonie K. Lesaux. "Breaking Down Words to Build Meaning: Morphology, Vocabulary, and Reading Comprehension in the Urban Classroom." *The Reading Teacher* 61 (2007): 134–144.

Lehr, Fran, Jean Osborn, and Elfrieda H. Hiebert. "Research-Based Practices in Early Reading Series: A Focus on Vocabulary." 2004. http://www.eric.ed.gov/?id=ED483190.

Mountain, Lee. "ROOTing Out Meaning: More Morphemic Analysis for Primary Pupils." *The Reading Teacher* 58 (2005): 742–749.

Nagy, William, Richard C. Anderson, Marlene Schommer, Judith Ann Scott, and Anne C. Stallman. "Morphological Families in the Internal Lexicon." *Reading Research Quarterly* 24 (1989): 262–282.

Nagy, William, and Judith Ann Scott. "Vocabulary Processes." In *Handbook of Reading Research*, Vol. III, edited by Michael L. Kamil, Peter B. Mosenthal, P. David Pearson, and Rebecca Barr, 269–284. Mahwah, NJ: Erlbaum, 2000.

Porter-Collier, I.M. "Teaching Vocabulary Through the Roots Approach in order to Increase Comprehension and Metacognition." Unpublished masters degree project. Akron OH: University of Akron, 2010.

Rasinski, Timothy, and Nancy Padak. *From Phonics to Fluency (3rd Edition)*. New York: Longman, 2013.

Rasinski, Timothy, Nancy Padak, Evangeline Newton, and Rick M. Newton. *Greek and Latin Roots: Keys to Building Vocabulary*. Huntington Beach, CA: Shell Educational Publishing, 2008.

Stahl, Steven A., and Marilyn M. Fairbanks. "The Effects of Vocabulary Instruction: A Model-Based Meta-Analysis." *Review of Educational Research* 56 (1986): 72–110.

Additional Practice Activities

Use the activities below to provide extra practice, to share with parents, or to differentiate instruction.

Card Games

The following card games can offer practice with roots:

Concentration (or Memory)

Select eight to ten words containing a root or base. Make double sets of word cards for each (or put the word and its definition on separate cards). Shuffle the cards and put them facedown on a table. Players take turns trying to make matches. The player with the most cards wins the game.

Go Fish

Select four to six bases. For each, create a set of four words (see Appendix E for related words). Students use these to play "Go Fish."

Word War

Provide words containing several roots and related terms written on cards. Play the card game "War" with them. Each player turns up a card. The person whose card a) comes first in alphabetical order, b) has more letters, or c) has more syllables wins the round as long as he or she can say both words and their meanings. If the words are similar, players draw again and the same rules as before apply. The player who wins this "war" takes all of the cards. A player who gets all of his or her partner's cards wins the game.

Word Games

The following word games can offer practice with roots:

List-Group-Label or Word Webs

Provide a root. Ask students to brainstorm words containing the root. Write these on the board or chart paper. Then ask small groups to work with the words by:

- listing related terms and providing labels for them.
- developing a graphic, such as a web, that shows how the words are related.

Additional Practice Activities *(cont.)*

Root Word Riddles

Who doesn't enjoy the brain-teasing process of trying to solve a riddle? This strategy invites students to create and guess riddles with words from the same base. Give pairs of students a list of words that contain the targeted base. Each pair's job is to devise riddles for other students to solve. (You may want to model riddle creation for students.) Example:

invisible

1. I have four syllables.
2. I have two word parts.
3. One part means "not."
4. The other part means "see."
5. I mean "not perceptible to the human eye."

What am I?

Sketch to Stretch

Provide words written on slips of paper and distribute them to students. Ask students to sketch something that reveals the word meaning. Then have them share these with others who try to guess what they have drawn.

Wordo

This vocabulary version of Bingo is a wonderful way for students to play with new words they are learning. List 24 words containing the targeted root(s) on the board. Duplicate a Wordo card found on pages 127–128 and in the Digital Resources (3x3wordomatrix. pdf and 4x4wordomatrix.pdf) for each student. Ask each student to choose a free box and mark it. Then have them write one of the words from the board in each of the remaining boxes. Students choose whatever box they wish for each word.

Now call a clue for each word: the definition, a synonym, an antonym, or a sentence with the target word deleted. Students figure out the correct target word and then draw an *X* through it. (If you want to clear the sheets and play again, use small scraps of paper or other small items to mark the squares.) When a student has *X*s or markers in a row, a column, a diagonal, or four corners, he or she can call out "Wordo!"

Additional Practice Activities *(cont.)*

Word Skits

List eight to ten words containing the targeted root(s) on the board. Divide students into teams of three to four. Each team chooses one word and writes its definition on an index card. Working together, they create a skit or situation that shows the meaning of the word. The skit is performed without words. Classmates try to guess the word being shown. Once the word is correctly identified, the definition is read out loud.

Word Sorts

Select about ten words containing the targeted root(s). Put the words on individual cards or slips of paper. (If you are introducing Word Sorts to students, you may also want to put the words on a blank transparency and cut them apart so that you can demonstrate the process of sorting the words.)

Provide one set of word cards to each pair of students. Ask students to group the words. Remind them that they will be asked to explain their groupings. Some criteria for grouping include:

a. presence/absence of a prefix or suffix

b. number of syllables

c. presence/absence of a long-vowel sound (in general, or a particular long-vowel sound)

After a few minutes, invite students to tell about one of their groups, the words contained in it and the reason for putting them together. If time permits, ask students to sort the same set of words repeatedly (e.g., by presence/absence of word part, or by number of syllables). Each sort provides students another opportunity to think about both the words and their component parts.

Word Spokes

Duplicate a Word Spokes Chart found on page 129 and in the Digital Resources (wordspokeschart.pdf) for each student or pair of students. Put the targeted root on the board. Have students put the targeted root in the center. Ask students to identify enough words containing the root to complete the chart. You may want to ask students to add sentences or illustrations of selected words, as well. Conclude the activity with sharing.

Be the Bard

Have students combine the roots covered in the book in different ways to create new words (e.g., *hemiport, motiport*), in much the same way that Shakespeare created new words such as *bedroom* and *premeditated*.

3 x 3 Wordo Matrix

4 x 4 Wordo Matrix

Word Spokes Chart

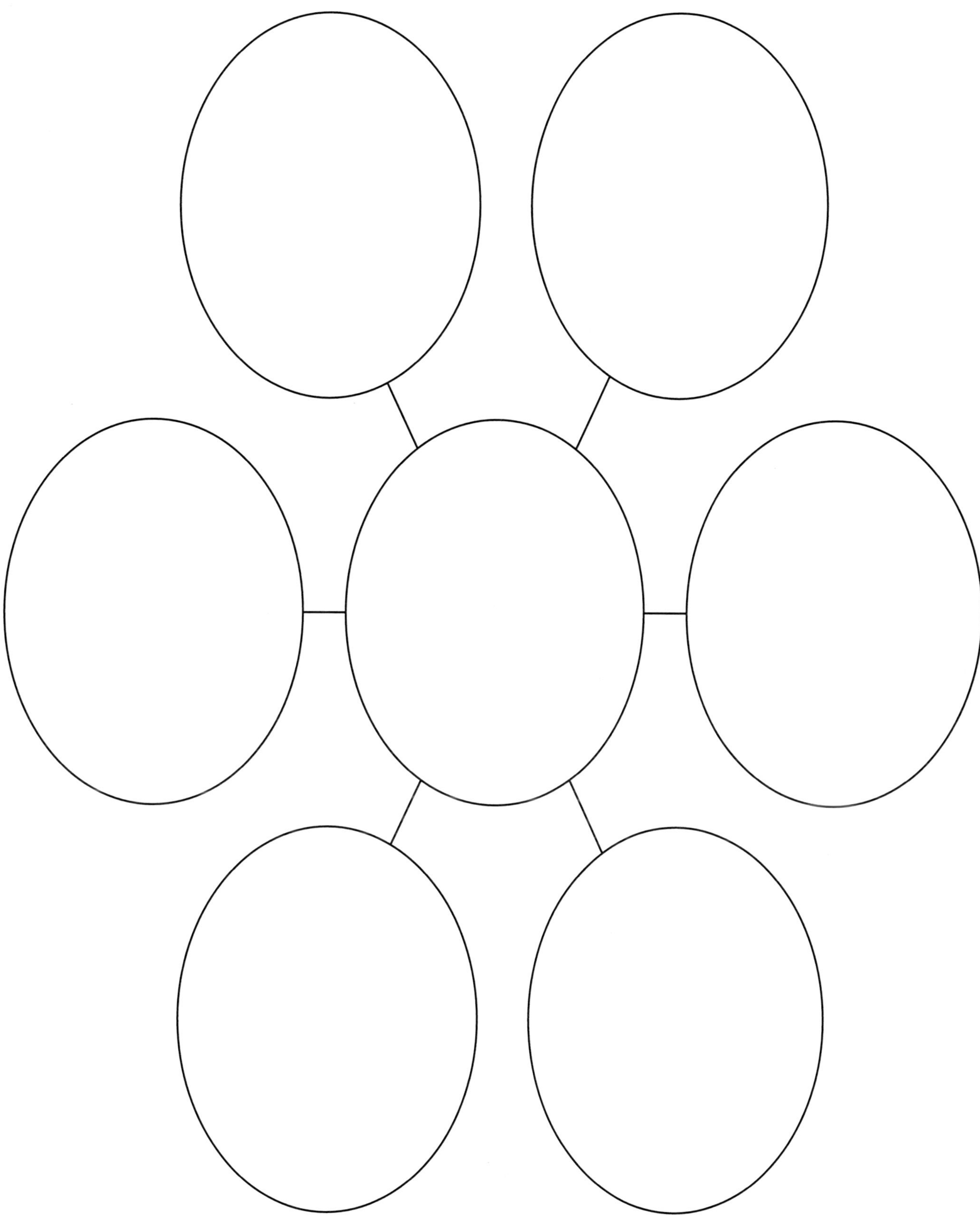

Name: ________________________________ Date: ______________

Unit I–Lesson 1:

Negative Prefix *in-*

Directions: The words on the chart have the negative prefix *in-*, which means "not." Write the letter from the Definition Bank for the correct word.

Word	Prefix Means	Base Word Is	Definition
1. incorrect			
2. ineligible			
3. incomplete			
4. inequality			
5. incredible			

Definition Bank

A. hard to believe

B. unfinished

C. wrong

D. not being equal

E. not entitled or qualified for something

Name: ______________________________ Date: ______________

Unit 1–Lesson 2:
Prefix co-, con-

Directions: The words on the chart have the prefix *co-*, *con-*, which means "with," "together." Write the letter from the Definition Bank for the correct word.

Word	Prefix Means	Base Is/Means	Definition
1. coauthor			
2. cooperate			
3. contract		*tract-* = pull, draw, drag	
4. congregation		*greg-* = flock, herd	
5. construct		*struct-* = build	

Definition Bank

A. to work with others and get along

B. to build or put together

C. a group of people who flock together for a ceremony

D. to write with someone else

E. a formal agreement

Name: ______________________________ Date: ______________

Unit 1—Lesson 3:

Prefixes *com-* and *col-*

Directions: The words on the chart have the prefixes *com-* or *col-,* which mean "with," or "together." Write the letter from the Definition Bank for the correct word.

Word	Prefix Means	Base Means	Definition
1. collide		*lid-* = strike, crash	
2. compose		*pos-* = put, place	
3. collection		*lect-* = choose, gather	
4. compete		*pet-* = seek, pursue	
5. compress		*press-* = press, squeeze	

Definition Bank

A. a group of objects, like stamps or coins, that are kept together

B. to clash or crash together

C. to squeeze together or smash down

D. to strive against others to win or get to a goal

E. to make or form by combining things

Name: ______________________________________ Date: _______________

Unit I—Lesson 4:

Base *port-*

Directions: The words on the chart have the base *port-,* which means "carry." An *X* means that the word has no prefix. Write the letter from the Definition Bank for the correct word.

Word	Prefix Means	Base Means	Definition
1. export	*ex-* = out		
2. transport	*trans-* = across, change		
3. porter	X		
4. portage	X		
5. deport	*de-* = down, off of		

Definition Bank

A. to carry a boat or canoe from one river or stream to another

B. to send a person out of the country, to banish or expel by legal means

C. to carry goods out of a country or a region

D. a person who carries luggage

E. to carry goods across an area from one place to another

Name: ______________________________ Date: ______________

Unit I—Lesson 5:

Bases *mov-*, *mot-*, and *mobil-*

Directions: The words on the chart have the bases *mov-*, *mot-*, or *mobil-*, which mean "move." An *X* means that the word has no prefix. Write the letter from the Definition Bank for the correct word.

Word	Prefix Means	Base Means	Definition
1. promote	*pro-* = forward, ahead		
2. commotion	*com-* = with, together		
3. mobile	X		
4. motion	X		
5. remove	*re-* = back, again		

Definition Bank

A. movement; also, a proposal made in a meeting

B. to move a student on to the next grade

C. disturbance or confusion; a hubbub

D. to take away

E. able to move, able to be moved

Name: ____ Date: ________________

Unit II–Lesson 1:

Prefixes e- and ex-

Directions: The words on the chart have the prefixes *e-* or *ex-*, which mean "out." Write the letter from the Definition Bank for the correct word.

Word	Prefix Means	Base Means	Definition
1. explode		*plod-* = burst	
2. exclaim		*claim-* = shout, cry	
3. extend		*tend-* = stretch	
4. erode		*rod-* = chew, gnaw	
5. exclude		*clud-* = shut, close	

Definition Bank

A. to shut out from the group

B. to make longer

C. to shout

D. to wear away gradually

E. to blow up

Name: ______________________________ Date: ______________

Unit II–Lesson 2:

Directional Prefix *in-*

Directions: The words on the chart have the directional prefix *in-*, which means "in," "on," "into." Write the letter from the Definition Bank for the correct word.

Word	Prefix Means	Base Means	Definition
1. inspect		*spect-* = look, watch	
2. inflate		*flat-* = blow	
3. inflammable		*flam-* = flame	
4. inhale		*hal-* = breathe	
5. induct		*duct-* = lead	

Definition Bank

A. to fill with air, to puff up

B. to admit into a club, to draft into the army

C. to take a breath

D. to study carefully

E. something that could burst into flames

Name: ______________________________ Date: ______________

Unit II–Lesson 3:

Prefix sub-

Directions: The words on the chart have the prefix *sub-*, which means "under," "below." Write the letter from the Definition Bank for the correct word.

Word	Prefix Means	Base Means	Definition
1. submerge		*merg-* = plunge, dip	
2. subterranean		*terra-* = earth	
3. subnormal		*norm-* = norm	
4. subside		*sid-* = sit, settle	
5. subtract		*tract-* = pull, draw, drag	

Definition Bank

A. to calm down, to settle down; (of flood waters) to settle at a lower level

B. to take away

C. to dive or fall under water

D. below average, less than normal, falling below the norm

E. underground

Name: ______________________________ Date: ______________

Unit II–Lesson 4:

Prefixes *semi-* and *hemi-*

Directions: The words on the chart have the prefixes *semi-* or *hemi-*, which mean "half" or "partial." Write the letter from the Definition Bank for the correct word.

Word	Prefix Means	Base Means	Definition
1. semiannual		*annu-* = year	
2. semiaquatic		*aqua-* = water	
3. hemisphere		*sphere-* = globe	
4. semicircular		*circl-* = circle	
5. semiprecious		*preci-* = value	

Definition Bank

A. living in water part of the time

B. gems that have high value but are not as costly as some gems

C. shaped like a half-circle

D. one half of the globe of Earth

E. lasting or happening every half year (every six months)

Name: ______________________________ Date: ______________

Unit II–Lesson 5:

Base *vid-, vis-*

Directions: The words on the chart have the base *vid-, vis-*, which means "see." An *X* means that the word has no prefix. Write the letter from the Definition Bank for the correct word.

Word	Prefix Means	Base Means	Definition
1. revision	*re-* = back, again		
2. provisions	*pro-* = forward, ahead		
3. visit	X		
4. visor	X		
5. evident	*e-* = out, very		

Definition Bank

A. a change or reform

B. the front of a baseball cap

C. supplies or plans for future needs

D. clear to see or to understand; obvious

E. to go and see a person or place

Name: ______________________________ Date: ______________

Unit III—Lesson 1:

Numerical Prefixes *uni-* and *unit-*

Directions: The words on the chart have the prefixes *uni-* or *unit-*, which means "one," "single." An *X* means that *uni- or unit-* is the base. Write the letter from the Definition Bank for the correct word.

Word	Prefix Means	Base Means	Definition
1. unicycle		*cycle-* = wheel, circle	
2. unison		*son-* = sound, voice	
3. unify		*fy-* = do, make	
4. unit		X	
5. uniform		*form-* = form, shape	

Definition Bank

A. to shape into a single whole, to make one

B. a one-wheeled vehicle

C. a single item, a single quantity

D. a single suit of clothing worn by different people; also, smooth and regular

E. one sound from many instruments or voices

Name: ______________________________ Date: ______________

Unit III–Lesson 2:

Numerical Prefix *bi-*

Directions: The words on the chart have the prefix *bi-*, which means "two." Write the letter from the Definition Bank for the correct word.

Word	Prefix Means	Base Means	Definition
1. bisect		*sect-* = slice, cut	
2. biannual		*annu-* = year	
3. bilateral		*later-* = side	
4. bilingual		*lingu-* = tongue, language	
5. biped		*ped-* = foot, leg	

Definition Bank

A. a person who can speak two languages; something written in two languages

B. happening two times a year

C. to cut in half

D. two-sided, as in an agreement

E. a creature that walks on two legs

Name: ______________________________ Date: ______________

Unit III–Lesson 3:

Numerical Prefix *tri-*

Directions: The words on the chart have the prefix *tri-*, which means "three." Write the letter from the Definition Bank for the correct word.

Word	Prefix Means	Base Means	Definition
1. trisect		*sect-* = cut, slice	
2. tripod		*pod-* = foot, leg	
3. tricycle		cycle = wheel, circle	
4. triangular		*angl-*, *angul-* = angle	
5. trilingual		*lingu-* = language, tongue	

Definition Bank

A. three sided; having three angles and three corresponding sides

B. a three-legged stand

C. a three-wheeler

D. speaking three languages; written in three languages

E. to divide into three equal parts

Name: ______________________________ Date: ______________

Unit III–Lesson 4:
Numerical Prefixes *quadr-* and *quart-*

Directions: The words on the chart have the prefixes *quadr-* or *quart-*, which mean "four" or "one-fourth." An *X* means that *quadr-* or *quart-* is the base. Write the letter from the Definition Bank for the correct word.

Word	Prefix Means	Base Means	Definition
1. quadrangular		*angl-*, *angul-* = angle	
2. quadrisect		*sect-* = cut, slice	
3. quarter		X	
4. quadrennial		*enni-* = year(s)	
5. quart		X	

Definition Bank

A. one-fourth of a dollar

B. one-fourth of a gallon

C. lasting four years; happening every four years

D. describing an object with four angles and four sides

E. to divide into four equal parts

Name: ______________________________ Date: ________________

Unit III–Lesson 5:

Numerical Prefix cent-

Directions: The words on the chart have the prefix *cent-*, which means "one hundred" or "$\frac{1}{100}$." An *X* means that *cent-* is the base. Write the letter from the Definition Bank for the correct word.

Word	Prefix Means	Base Means	Definition
1. centennial		*enni-* = year(s)	
2. centigrade		*grad-* = step, degree	
3. centipede		*ped-* = foot, leg	
4. centimeter		*meter-* = measure, meter	
5. cent		X	

Definition Bank

A. having 100 degrees

B. a 100-year anniversary

C. $\frac{1}{100}$ of a dollar; one penny

D. $\frac{1}{100}$ of a meter

E. an insect with 100 hundred legs

Answer Key

Unit I–Social Studies

Lesson 1: Negative Prefix *in-* (page 130)

1. C
2. E
3. B
4. D
5. A

Lesson 2: Prefix co-, *con-* (page 131)

1. D
2. A
3. E
4. C
5. B

Lesson 3: Prefixes *com-* and *col-* (page 132)

1. B
2. E
3. A
4. D
5. C

Lesson 4: Base *port-* (page 133)

1. C
2. E
3. D
4. A
5. B

Lesson 5: Bases *mov-*, *mot-*, and *mobil-* (page 134)

1. B
2. C
3. E
4. A
5. D

Unit II–Science

Lesson 1: Prefixes *e-* and *ex-* (page 135)

1. E
2. C
3. B
4. D
5. A

Lesson 2: Directional Prefix *in-* (page 136)

1. D
2. A
3. E
4. C
5. B

Lesson 3: Prefix *sub-* (page 137)

1. C
2. E
3. D
4. A
5. B

Lesson 4: Prefixes *semi-* and *hemi-* (page 138)

1. E
2. A
3. D
4. C
5. B

Lesson 5: Base *vid-, vis-* (page 139)

1. A
2. C
3. E
4. B
5. D

Answer Key *(cont.)*

Unit III—Math

Lesson 1: Numerical Prefixes *uni-* and *unit-* (page 140)

1. B
2. E
3. A
4. C
5. D

Lesson 2: Numerical Prefix *bi-* (page 141)

1. C
2. B
3. D
4. A
5. E

Lesson 3: Numerical Prefix *tri-* (page 142)

1. E
2. B
3. C
4. A
5. D

Lesson 4: Numerical Prefixes *quadr-* and *quart-* (page 143)

1. D
2. E
3. A
4. C
5. B

Lesson 5: Numerical Prefix *cent-* (page 144)

1. B
2. A
3. E
4. D
5. C

Sample Content-Area Words

in- (negative) = "not"

inaccurate	**indecent**	**inexact**
inactive	**indefensible**	**inexcusable**
inadmissible	**independent**	**inexpensive**
inalienable	**independence**	**inhumane**
inappropriate	**indifferent**	**inoffensive**
incapable	**indirect**	**insufficient**
incompetent	**indisputable**	**intolerant**
incomplete	**indivisible**	**invalid**
inconclusive	**ineffective**	**invisible**
inconvenient	**ineligible**	**involuntary**
incorrect		

co-, con- = "with," "together"

coalition	**conflict**	**conspire** conspiracy conspiring conspired conspirator
coauthor	**congress**	**constituent**
coexist	**cooperate** cooperated cooperating cooperation	**continent**
cohabitate	**conflict**	**convention**
confederate	**conservation**	**coworker**
conference		

Sample Content-Area Words *(cont.)*

com-, col- = "with," "together"

collaborate	**college** collegiate collegian	**commonwealth**	**communism**
collateral		**commune** communal	**community**
collect collecting collected collector collective	**combine** combination	**communicate** communicating communicated communicator	**compact**
	common commoner		**compromise** compromised compromising

port- = "carry"

airport	**export** exported exporting exporter	**port**	**transport** transportation transported transporter
comport		**porter**	
deport deported deportation, deporting	**import** imported importer importation	**portage**	
		report reports reporter reported reporting	

Sample Content-Area Words *(cont.)*

mov-, mot-, mobil- = "move"

automobile

commotion

immobile

locomotive
locomotion

mobilize
mobilization
upward mobility

motion

motivate
motivated
motivator
motivated
motivating

motive

motor
motorize

move
mover
moved
moving

movement

promote
promotion
promoted
promoter
promoting

remove
removed
removal
removing

e-, ex- = "out"

exact
exacted
exacting

examine
examining
examined
examination
examiner

excavate
excavation
excavating
excavator
excavated

excision
excise
excising
excised

excursion

exert
exertion
exerted
exerting

exfoliate

exhale
exhaling
exhaled
exhalation

exhaust
exhausting
exhausted
exhaustion

exhume
exhuming
exhumed
exhumation

exist
existed
existing
existence

exit
exited
exiting

expand
expanded
expanding
expansion

expel
expelling
expelled

expend
expended
expending

experiment
experimenting
experimented
experimentation
experimenter

expire
expired
expiring
expiration

explode
explosion
exploding
exploded

explore
explorer
explored
exploring
exploration

expose
exposure
exposing
exposed

exterminate
exterminator
exterminated
exterminating

extinct
extinction

extract
extracting
extracted

extrude
extrusion
extruder
extruding
extruded

Sample Content-Area Words *(cont.)*

in- (directional) = "in," "on," "into"

incise
incisor
incised
incising

incline
inclination
inclined
inclining

indicate
indication
indicated
indicating
indicator

indigenous

inductive
induce
inducing
induced

inert

infect
infection
infecting
infected

infiltration

inflammable

inflate
inflation
inflated
inflating

infuse
infusion
infused
infusing

ingest
ingested
ingesting

ingredient

ingrowth

inhabit
inhabitant

inhale
inhalation
inhaling
inhaled

inherit
inherited
inheriting
inheritance

innate

inoculate
inoculation
inoculated
inoculating

insect
insecticide

instinct

intake

internal

intestine
intestinal

invade
invader
invasion
invaded
invasive
invading

Sample Content-Area Words *(cont.)*

sub- = "under," "below"

subaerial

subaquatic

subatmospheric

subcelestial

subclass

subcortex

subhuman

submarine

subglacial

submerge
submerging
submerged

suboceanic

subsolar

subsonic

substance
substantive

substruct

subsurface

subsume
subsuming
subsumed

subterranean

subtract
subtracted
subtracting

subzero

semi-, hemi- = "half," "partial"

hemicycle

hemihydrate
hemihydrated

hemisphere
hemispheric
hemispherical

semiabstract

semicircle
semicircular

semiconductor

semiconsciousness

semidarkness

semifinal

semiformed

semiliquid

semilunar

semiliquid

semiprecious

semiskilled

semisolid

semispherical

semitransparent

semitropical

Sample Content-Area Words *(cont.)*

vid-, vis- = "see"

evident
evidence

envision
envisioning
envisioned

improvise
improvised
improvising
improvisation

invisible

nonvisual

provide
provisions
provident
providence
Providence

revise
revision
revising
revised

revisit
revisited
revisiting

supervise
supervisor
supervision
supervising
supervised

televise
televised
televising
television

unrevised

unsupervised

video
videography

visible

vision

visit
visiting
visited
visitor

visual acuity

visualize

uni-, unit- = "one," "single"

E Pluribus Unum
one out of many

unicelled
unicellular

unicolor
unicolored

unicorn

unicycle

unification

uniform
uniformed

unify
unifying
unified

union

unison

unit

unite
united
uniting

Sample Content-Area Words *(cont.)*

bi- = "two"

biannual

bicameral

bicentennial

biceps

bicultural

bicuspid

bicycle
bicycling

bidirectional

biennial

biennium

bifocals
bifocal

bilingual
bilingualism

bimonthly

binocular
binoculars

biped
bipeds

biplane

bisect
bisected
bisecting
bisection

bivalve

biweekly

combine
combination

tri- = "three"

triangle
triangular

triathlete

triathlon

Tribeca
[Triangle Below Canal]

triceps

triceratops

tricolor
tricolored

tricuspid

tricycle
tricycle
tricycling

trifocal
trifocals

trilingual
trilingualism

trilogy
trilogies

trimester

trimonthly

trio

triplets

triple
tripled
tripling

triplane

triplicate

tripod

Tripoli

trisect
trisected
trisecting

triweekly

Sample Content-Area Words *(cont.)*

quadr-, quart- = "four," "one-fourth"

quadrangle	**quadruple** quadrupling quadrupled	**quarterback**
quadrant	**quart**	**quarterfinal**
quadrennial	**quarter** quartered	**quartet**
quadrilateral		**quartot**
quadrisect		

cent- = "one hundred," "one one-hundredth"

bicentennial	**centigrade**	**century** centuries
cent cents	**centigram**	**percent** percentage percentile
centenarian	**centiliter**	**tricentennial**
centennial	**centimeter**	
	centurion	

Flashcards

in- (negative)

co- and *con-*

Flashcards *(cont.)*

"not"

"with," "together"

Flashcards *(cont.)*

com- **and** ***col-***

port-

Flashcards *(cont.)*

"with," "together"

"carry"

Flashcards *(cont.)*

mov-, mot-,
and *mobil-*

e-* and *ex-

Flashcards *(cont.)*

“move”

“out”

Flashcards *(cont.)*

in-
(directional)

sub-

Flashcards *(cont.)*

"in," "on,"
"into"

"under,"
"below"

Flashcards *(cont.)*

semi- **and** ***hemi-***

vid- **and** ***vis-***

Flashcards *(cont.)*

"half,"
"partial"

"see"

Flashcards *(cont.)*

uni-* and *unit-

bi-

Flashcards *(cont.)*

“one,” “single”

“two”

Flashcards *(cont.)*

tri-

quadr- and quart-

Flashcards *(cont.)*

"three"

"four,"
"one-fourth"

Flashcards *(cont.)*

Flashcards *(cont.)*

"one hundred," "one one-hundredth"

Contents of the Digital Resources

Accessing the Digital Resources

The Digital Resources can be downloaded by following these steps:

1. Go to **www.tcmpub.com/digital**
2. Use the ISBN number to redeem the Digital Resources.

3. Respond to the question using the book.
4. Follow the prompts on the Content Cloud website to sign in or create a new account.
5. The redeemed content will now be on your My Content screen. Click on the product to look through the Digital Resources. All files can be downloaded, while some files can also be previewed, opened, and shared.

Activity Sheets		
Page	**Activity Sheet**	**Filename**
22–23	About the Root: Negative Prefix *in-*	abrnegativeprefixin.pdf
24	Divide and Conquer: Negative Prefix *in-*	dcnegativeprefixin.pdf
25	Making Connections: *Not* Word Sort	notwordsort.pdf
28–29	About the Root: Prefix *co-, con-*	abrprefixescoandcon.pdf
30	Divide and Conquer: Prefix *co-, con-*	dcprefixescoandcon.pdf
31	Making Connections: Draw It!	drawit.pdf
34–35	About the Root: Prefixes *com-* and *col-*	abrprefixescomandcol.pdf
36	Divide and Conquer: Prefixes *com-* and *col-*	dcprefixescomandcol.pdf
37	Making Connections: *con-* or *com-*?	conorcom.pdf
40–41	About the Root: Base *port-*	abrbaseport.pdf
42	Divide and Conquer: Base *port-*	dcbaseport.pdf
43	Making Connections: Riddle Me This	riddlemethis.pdf
46–47	About the Root: Bases *mov-*, *mot-*, and *mobil-*	abrbasesmovmotandmobil.pdf
48	Divide and Conquer: Bases *mov-*, *mot-*, and *mobil-*	dcbasesmovmotandmobil.pdf
49	Making Connections: Moving or Not Moving?	movingornotmoving.pdf

Contents of the Digital Resources *(cont.)*

Activity Sheets		
Page	**Activity Sheet**	**Filename**
50-51	Review: Social Studies Crossword Puzzle	socialstudiesreview.pdf
54–55	About the Root: Prefixes *e-* and *ex-*	abrprefixeseandex.pdf
56	Divide and Conquer: Prefixes *e-* and *ex-*	dcprefixeseandex.pdf
57	Making Connections: Guess My Picture!	guessmypicture.pdf
60–61	About the Root: Directional Prefix *in-*	abrdirectionalprefixin.pdf
62	Divide and Conquer: Directional Prefix *in-*	dcdirectionalprefixin.pdf
63	Making Connections: Is It "In" or Is It "Not"?	isitinorisitnot.pdf
66–67	About the Root: Prefix *sub-*	abrprefixsub.pdf
68	Divide and Conquer: Prefix *sub-*	dcprefixsub.pdf
69	Making Connections: *Sub-* Words	subwords.pdf
72–73	About the Root: Prefixes *semi-* and *hemi-*	abrprefixessemiandhemi.pdf
74	Divide and Conquer: Prefixes *semi-* and *hemi-*	dcprefixessemiandhemi.pdf
75	Making Connections: Scrambles	scrambles.pdf
78–79	About the Root: Base *vid-*, *vis-*	abrbasesvidandvis.pdf
80	Divide and Conquer: Base *vid-*, *vis-*	dcbasesvidandvis.pdf
81	Making Connections: Riddle Time!	riddletime.pdf
82-83	Review: Science Crossword Puzzle	sciencereview.pdf
86–87	About the Root: Numerical Prefixes *uni-* and *unit-*	abrnumericalprefixesuniandunit.pdf
88	Divide and Conquer: Numerical Prefixes *uni-* and *unit-*	dcnumericalprefixesuniandunit.pdf
89	Making Connections: *Uni-* Scramble	uniscramble.pdf
92–93	About the Root: Numerical Prefix *bi-*	abrnumericalprefixbi.pdf
94	Divide and Conquer: Numerical Prefix *bi-*	dcnumericalprefixbi.pdf
95	Making Connections: Two or Not Two?	twoornottwo.pdf
98–99	About the Root: Numerical Prefix *tri-*	abrnumericalprefixtri.pdf
100	Divide and Conquer: Numerical Prefix *tri-*	dcnumericalprefixtri.pdf
101	Making Connections: *Tri-* Riddles	tririddles.pdf
104–105	About the Root: Numerical Prefixes *quadr-* and *quart-*	abrnumericalprefixesquadrandquart.pdf
106	Divide and Conquer: Numerical Prefixes *quadr-* and *quart-*	dcnumericalprefixesquadrandquart.pdf
107	Making Connections: Draw Four	drawfour.pdf
110–111	About the Root: Numerical Prefix *cent-*	abrnumericalprefixcent.pdf
112	Divide and Conquer: Numerical Prefix *cent-*	dcnumericalprefixcent.pdf

Contents of the Digital Resources *(cont.)*

Activity Sheets		
Page	**Activity Sheet**	**Filename**
113	Making Connections: Five Scramble	fivescramble.pdf
114	Review: Magic Square Math	mathematicsreview.pdf

Additional Resources		
Page	**Additional Resource**	**Filename**
17	Standards	standards.pdf
127	3 x 3 Wordo Matrix	3x3wordomatrix.pdf
128	4 x 4 Wordo Matrix	4x4wordomatrix.pdf
129	Word Spokes Chart	wordspokeschart.pdf
130–146	Additional Assessment Activities	additionalassessments.pdf
147–154	Sample Content-Area Words	samplewordlists.pdf
155–170	Flashcards	flashcards.pdf

Notes

Notes

Notes